FIVE PLAYS

BY

John Mortimer

THE DOCK BRIEF
WHAT SHALL WE TELL CAROLINE?
I SPY
LUNCH HOUR
COLLECT YOUR HAND BAGGAGE

METHUEN & CO LTD
11 NEW FETTER LANE · LONDON EC4

First published in this edition in 1970
The Dock Brief
What Shall We Tell Caroline?
I Spy
© 1958 by John Mortimer
Lunch Hour
Collect Your Hand Baggage
© 1960 by John Mortimer (Productions) Ltd
Printed in Great Britain
by Cox & Wyman Ltd, Fakenham, Norfolk
SBN 416 12760 6 Hardback
416 12770 3 Paperback

Contents

Introduction

Comedy, I remember saying when these plays were first published, is the only thing worth writing in this despairing world. Ten years later the world has offered no call for a change of attitude. It may be that only in the most secure and optimistic ages can good tragedies be written. Our present situation, stumbling into a misty future filled with uncertainty and mistrust, is far too serious to be described in terms that give us no opportunity to laugh.

Perhaps, when these plays were written, in the late fifties and early sixties, we had not yet been entirely liberated into anarchic farce. The Macmillan era was a time for low comedy in high places. Pre-war attitudes still lingered. The middle-aged formed hopeless and isolated pockets of resistance, in law courts and seaside hotels and private schools, to that new and stronger generation, nurtured on free orange juice, for whom the Battle of Britain was to become about as interesting an event as the Relief of Mafeking.

The Prime Minister himself set the tone, with a vague watery eye and straggling moustache, with a voice made to go with old tweed hats and gum boots, he was to find his great British reverie shattered by a volley of slammed bedroom doors. I think Macmillan and Morgenhall, the totally unsuccessful barrister in *Dock Brief*, shared the same innocence. Their fantasies were similar, and they were equally hurt when they stubbed their toes on awkward and protruding bits of life.

So I have attempted, in these comedies, to chart the tottering course of British middle-class attitudes in decline. My choice of such a subject was dictated by myself, my childhood and such education as I was able to gather from the shell-shocked veterans of the 1914 war who regarded, at my prep school, every boy as at least part Hun. Critics often talk as if writers had a wide degree of choice in the sort of play they produce, as if we could sit down in the morning and say 'what about telling a social epic on the Thirty Years' War for Nottingham this morning?' The truth, as I have found it, is that you can only work within that narrow seam which penetrates to the depths of your past.

For that reason, I have always thought of the theatre as a writer's medium: and those performances in which the actors are encouraged to spontaneous utterance about life or the current political situation as finally dull. The extemporized words of actors, usually having been borrowed from some old play they once did in rep, are never the most profound. For me, there is no substitute for the long and lonely work of the writer, writing words which must be delivered with total accuracy if the whole mood and colour of the play is not to vanish in a well-meaning blur.

What these plays have in common is, that they are short. There are no rules in this business, and a play may be exactly as long as a piece of string. A play, in my view, is as apt a description for Harold Pinter's five-minute contribution to the revue *One to Another* as it is for *Man and Superman* or the entire *Dance of Death*. No one complains about a Rembrandt etching because it is not the same size as Frith's 'Derby Day', nor do those who visit the National Gallery to revive their spirits with a look at Cézanne's 'Old Lady' grumble because that experience has occupied them for less than two solid hours. The drama, however, is meant to neatly cover a certain well-defined period of our lives, based, I believe, on something as contemporary as the time it took to digest your dinner at the Trocadero and become hungry enough to face supper at the Savoy.

Films are likewise cursed, and for the worst commercial

reasons. Nothing under ninety minutes long can be resold to television. In order to squeeze in a sufficient number of interruptions concerned with floor polish, television sponsors will take no shorter. Even long films with intervals no doubt go for the sale of ice-creams. Short plays, without intervals, could only deprive the customers of those small hot gin and vermouths it is an impossible anxiety to struggle for in theatre bars anyway. In the future there may be a theatre of continuous short plays which could be seen in the same way as you might drop into an art gallery, stare at one or two pictures that take your eye, and depart as soon as your feet start to ache. At the moment, many plays we are glad to see arrive, linger on for their mandatory two hours, making conversation like those guests who have already rung for a mini-cab which, nerve-rackingly, never seems to turn up.

Whatever their length, I hope at least that each of these productions is a play. How do you distinguish a short play from a revue sketch? I think of a sketch as a caption, a one-line joke. A play, even if it lasts not more than five minutes, should be able to contain at least one life, with a character that can be conceived as stretching backwards and forwards in time, with an existence longer than those moments which actually take place on the stage. A play is a demonstration, in which an audience can recognize something about themselves. As with a picture, this can be achieved by a few lines in the right position.

I have to confess to a low threshold of boredom. At one distant Edinburgh Festival, I recall that Kenneth Tynan named us the 'half-time Mortimers', and though I have often been with Saint Joan when she picked out the Dauphin, I have not always been among those present when she made her posthumous return to his sleepless bedroom. I have some sympathy with Sir Charles Dilke, who never saw more than one act of any play. He loved the theatre deeply, but enough, he no doubt felt, was as good as a feast. I have even more

sympathy with that anonymous and candid M.P. who fell
asleep during his own maiden speech. There is something a
little desperate about seeing a character, who has occupied a
year of your life, coming through the door at the opening of
the third act. 'What you *again*?' you may be inclined to mutter,
gripping the pen to provide him with another, scarcely deserved
page of dialogue. In a one act play, the enthusiasm has no
time to die. The only rule I have found to have any meaning in
writing is to try and not bore yourself.

24.11.69   John Mortimer

The Dock Brief

First produced by the BBC Third Programme on May 12, 1957. The cast was as follows:

MORGENHALL *Michael Hordern*
FOWLE *David Kosoff*

Produced by Nesta Pain

On September 16, 1957 the play was produced on BBC television with the same cast and producer.

Michael Codron with David Hall (for Talbot Productions Ltd.) presented the play in a double bill (with *What Shall We Tell Caroline?*) at the Lyric Opera House, Hammersmith, on April 9, 1958, and on May 20, 1958 at the Garrick Theatre. The cast was as follows:

MORGENHALL *Michael Hordern*
FOWLE *Maurice Denham*

Directed by Stuart Burge
Designed by Disley Jones

Scene One

A cell. The walls are grey and fade upwards into the shadows, so that the ceiling is not seen, and it might even be possible to escape upwards. The door is right. Back stage is a high, barred window through which the sky looks very blue. Under the window is a stool. Against the left wall is a bench with a wooden cupboard next to it. On the cupboard a wash basin, a towel and a Bible.

A small fat prisoner is standing on the stool on tip toes, his hands in his pockets. His eyes are on the sky.

Bolts shoot back. The door opens. MORGENHALL *strides in. He is dressed in a black gown and bands, an aged barrister with the appearance of a dusty vulture. He speaks off stage, to the warder.*

MORGENHALL (*to an unseen warder*). Is this where . . . you keep Mr Fowle? Good, excellent. Then leave us alone like a kind fellow. Would you mind closing the door? These old places are so draughty.

The door closes. The bolts shoot back.

Mr Fowle . . . Where are you, Mr Fowle? Not escaped, I pray. Good Heavens man, come down. Come down, Mr Fowle.

He darts at him and there is a struggle as he pulls down the bewildered FOWLE.

I haven't hurt you?
FOWLE: *negative sounding noise.*

I was suddenly anxious. A man in your unfortunate position. Desperate measures. And I couldn't bear to lose you . . . No, don't stand up. It's difficult for you without braces, or a belt,

I can see. And no tie, no shoe-laces. I'm so glad they're looking after you. You must forgive me if I frightened you just a little, Mr Fowle. It was when I saw you up by that window. . . .

FOWLE (*a hoarse and sad voice*). Epping Forest.

MORGENHALL. What did your say?

FOWLE. I think you can see Epping Forest.

MORGENHALL. No doubt you can. But why, my dear chap, why should you want to?

FOWLE. It's the home stretch.

MORGENHALL. Very well.

FOWLE. I thought I could get a glimpse of the green. Between the chimneys and that shed. . . .

FOWLE *starts to climb up again. A brief renewed struggle.*

MORGENHALL. No, get down. It's not wise to be up there, forever trying to look out. There's a draughty, sneeping wind. Treacherous.

FOWLE. Treacherous?

MORGENHALL. I'm afraid so. You never know what a mean, sneeping wind can do. Catch you by the throat, start a sneeze, then a dry tickle on the chest. I don't want anything to catch you like that before . . .

FOWLE. Before what?

MORGENHALL. You're much better sitting quietly down there in the warm. Just sit quietly and I'll introduce myself.

FOWLE. I am tired.

MORGENHALL. I'm Wilfred Morgenhall.

FOWLE. Wilfred?

MORGENHALL. Morgenhall. The barrister.

FOWLE. The barrister?

MORGENHALL. Perfectly so. . . .

FOWLE. I'm sorry.

MORGENHALL. Why?

FOWLE. A barrister. That's very bad.

MORGENHALL. I don't know. Why's it so bad?

FOWLE. When a gentleman of your stamp goes wrong. A long fall.

MORGENHALL. What can you mean?

FOWLE. Different for an individual like me. I only kept a small seed shop.

MORGENHALL. Seed shop? My poor fellow. We mustn't let this unfortunate little case confuse us. We're going to remain very calm, very lucid. We're going to come to important decisions. Now, do me a favour, Mr Fowle, no more seed shops.

FOWLE. Birdseed, of course. Individuals down our way kept birds mostly. Canaries and budgies. The budgies talked. Lot of lonely people down our way. They kept them for the talk.

MORGENHALL. Mr Fowle. I'm a barrister.

FOWLE. Tragic.

MORGENHALL. I know the law.

FOWLE. It's trapped you.

MORGENHALL. I'm here to help you.

FOWLE. We'll help each other.

Pause.

MORGENHALL (*laughs uncontrollably*). I see. Mr Fowle. I see where you've been bewildered. You think I'm in trouble as well. Then I've got good news for you at last. I'm free. Oh yes. I can leave here when I like.

FOWLE. You can?

MORGENHALL. The police are my friends.

FOWLE. They are?

MORGENHALL. And I've never felt better in my life. There now. That's relieved you, hasn't it? I'm not in any trouble.

FOWLE. Family all well?

MORGENHALL. I never married.

FOWLE. Rent paid up?

MORGENHALL. A week or two owing perhaps. Temporary lull in business. This case will end all that.

FOWLE. Which case?

MORGENHALL. Your case.

FOWLE. My . . . ?

MORGENHALL. Case.

FOWLE. Oh that – it's not important.

MORGENHALL. Not?

FOWLE. I don't care about it to any large extent. Not as at present advised.

MORGENHALL. Mr Fowle. How could you say that?

FOWLE. The flavour's gone out of it.

MORGENHALL. But we're only at the beginning.

FOWLE. I can't believe it's me concerned. . . .

MORGENHALL. But it is you, Mr Fowle. You mustn't let yourself forget that. You see, that's why you're here. . . .

FOWLE. I can't seem to bother with it.

MORGENHALL. Can you be so busy?

FOWLE. Slopping in, slopping out. Peering at the old forest. It fills in the day.

MORGENHALL. You seem, if I may say so, to have adopted an unpleasantly selfish attitude.

FOWLE. Selfish?

MORGENHALL. Dog in the manger.

FOWLE. In the?

MORGENHALL. Unenthusiastic.

FOWLE. You're speaking quite frankly, I well appreciate. . . .

MORGENHALL. I'm sorry, Fowle. You made me say it. There's so much of this about nowadays. There's so much ready made entertainment. Free billiards, National Health. Television. There's not the spirit abroad there used to be.

FOWLE. You feel that?

MORGENHALL. Whatever I've done I've always been mustard keen on my work. I've never lost the vision, Fowle. In all my disappointments I've never lost the love of the job.

FOWLE. The position in life you've obtained to.

MORGENHALL. Years of study I had to put in. It didn't just drop in my lap.

FOWLE. I've never studied. . . .

MORGENHALL. Year after year, Fowle, my window at college was alight until two a.m. There I sat among my books. I fed mainly on herrings. . . .

FOWLE. Lean years?

MORGENHALL. And black tea. No subsidized biscuits then, Fowle, no County Council tobacco, just work. . . .

FOWLE. Book work, almost entirely? I'm only assuming that, of course.

MORGENHALL. Want to hear some Latin?

FOWLE. Only if you have time.

MORGENHALL. Actus non sit reus nisi mens sit rea. Filius nullius. In flagrante delicto. Understand it?

FOWLE. I'm no scholar.

MORGENHALL. You most certainly are not. But I had to be, we all had to be in my day. Then we'd sit for the examinations, Mods, Smalls, Greats, Tripos, Little Goes, week after week, rowing men fainting, Indian students vomiting with fear, and no creeping out for a peep at the book under the pretext of a pump ship or getting a glance at the other fellow's celluloid cuff. . . .

FOWLE. That would be unheard of?

MORGENHALL. Then weeks, months of waiting. Nerve racking. Go up to the Lake District. Pace the mountains, play draughts, forget to huff. Then comes the fatal post-card.

FOWLE. What's it say?

MORGENHALL. Satisfied the examiners.

FOWLE. At last!

MORGENHALL. Don't rejoice so soon. True enough I felt I'd turned a corner, got a fur hood, bumped on the head with a

Bible. Bachelor of Law sounded sweet in my ears. I thought of celebrating, a few kindred spirits round for a light ale. Told the only lady in my life that in five years' time perhaps . . .

FOWLE. You'd arrived!

MORGENHALL. That's what I thought when they painted my name up on my London chambers. I sat down to fill in the time until they sent my first brief in a real case. I sat down to do the crossword puzzle while I waited. Five years later, Fowle, what was I doing . . . ?

FOWLE. A little charge of High Treason?

MORGENHALL. I was still doing the crossword puzzle.

FOWLE. But better at it?

MORGENHALL. Not much. Not very much. As the years pass there come to be clues you no longer understand.

FOWLE. So all that training?

MORGENHALL. Wasted. The talents rust.

FOWLE. And the lady?

MORGENHALL. Drove an ambulance in the 1914. A stray piece of shrapnel took her. I don't care to talk of it.

FOWLE. Tragic

MORGENHALL. What was?

FOWLE. Tragic my wife was never called up.

MORGENHALL. You mustn't talk like that, Fowle, your poor wife.

FOWLE. Don't let's carry on about me.

MORGENHALL. But we must carry on about you. That's what I'm here for.

FOWLE. You're here to?

MORGENHALL. Defend you.

FOWLE. Can't be done.

MORGENHALL. Why ever not?

FOWLE. I know who killed her.

MORGENHALL. Who?

FOWLE. Me.

Pause

MORGENHALL (*considerable thought before he says*). Mr Fowle,
I have all the respect in the world for your opinions, but we
must face this. You're a man of very little education. . . .

FOWLE. That's true.

MORGENHALL. One has only to glance at you. At those
curious lobes to your ears. At the line of your hair. At the
strange way your eyebrows connect in the middle, to see that
you're a person of very limited intelligence.

FOWLE. Agreed, quite frankly.

MORGENHALL. You think you killed your wife.

FOWLE. Seems to me.

MORGENHALL. Mr Fowle. Look at yourself objectively. On
questions of birdseed I have no doubt you may be infallible –
but on a vital point like this might you not be mistaken. . . .
Don't answer . . .

FOWLE. Why not, sir?

MORGENHALL. Before you drop the bomb of a reply, consider
who will be wounded. Are the innocent to suffer?

FOWLE. I only want to be honest.

MORGENHALL. But you're a criminal, Mr Fowle. You've
broken through the narrow fabric of honesty. You are free
to be kind, human, to do good.

FOWLE. But what I did to her . . .

MORGENHALL. She's passed, you know, out of your life.
You've set up new relationships. You've picked out me.

FOWLE. Picked out?

MORGENHALL. Selected.

FOWLE. But I didn't know. . . .

MORGENHALL. No, Mr Fowle. That's the whole beauty of it.
You didn't know me. You came to me under a system of
chance invented, like the football pools, to even out the
harsh inequality of a world where you have to deserve
success. You, Mr Fowle, are my first Dock Brief.

FOWLE. Your Dock?

MORGENHALL. Brief.

FOWLE. You couldn't explain?

MORGENHALL. Of course. Prisoners with no money and no friends exist. Luckily, you're one of them. They're entitled to choose any barrister sitting in Court to defend them. The barrister, however old, gets a brief, and is remunerated on a modest scale. Busy lawyers, wealthy lawyers, men with other interests, creep out of Court bent double when the Dock Brief is chosen. We regulars who are not busy sit on. I've been a regular for years. It's not etiquette, you see, even if you want the work, to wave at the prisoner, or whistle, or try to catch his eye by hoisting any sort of little flag.

FOWLE. Didn't know.

MORGENHALL. But you *can* choose the most advantageous seat. The seat any criminal would naturally point at. It's the seat under the window and for ten years my old friend Tuppy Morgan, bagged it each day at ten. He sat there, reading Horace, and writing to his innumerable aunts, and almost once a year a criminal pointed him out. Oh, Mr Fowle, Tuppy was a limpet on that seat. But this morning, something, possibly a cold, perhaps death, kept him indoors. So I had his place. And you spotted me, no doubt.

FOWLE. Spotted you?

MORGENHALL. My glass polished. My profile drawn and learned in front of the great window.

FOWLE. I never noticed.

MORGENHALL. But when they asked you to choose a lawyer?

FOWLE. I shut my eyes and pointed – I've picked horses that way, and football teams. Never did me any good, though, by any stretch of the imagination.

MORGENHALL. So even you, Mr Fowle, didn't choose me?

FOWLE. Not altogether.

MORGENHALL. The law's a haphazard business.

FOWLE. It does seem chancy.

MORGENHALL. Years of training, and then to be picked out like a football pool.

FOWLE. Don't take it badly sir.

MORGENHALL. Of course, you've been fortunate.

FOWLE. So unusual. I was never one to draw the free bird at Christmas, or guess the weight of the cake. Now I'm sorry I told you.

MORGENHALL. Never mind. You hurt me temporarily, Fowle, I must confess. It might have been kinder to have kept me in ignorance. But now it's done. Let's get down to business. And, Fowle –

FOWLE. Yes, sir.

MORGENHALL. Remember you're dealing with fellow man. A man no longer young. Remember the hopes I've pinned on you and try . . .

FOWLE. Try?

MORGENHALL. Try to spare me more pain.

FOWLE. I will, sir. Of course I will.

MORGENHALL. Now. Let's get our minds in order.

FOWLE. Sort things out?

MORGENHALL. Exactly. Now, this wife of yours.

FOWLE. Doris?

MORGENHALL. Doris. A bitter, unsympathetic woman?

FOWLE. She was always cheerful. She loved jokes.

MORGENHALL. Oh, Fowle. Do be very careful.

FOWLE. I will, sir. But if you'd known Doris. . . . She laughed harder than she worked. 'Thank God,' she'd say, 'for my old English sense of fun.'

MORGENHALL. What sort of jokes, Fowle, did this Doris appreciate?

FOWLE. All sorts. Pictures in the paper. Jokes on the wireless set. Laughs out of crackers, she'd keep them from Christmas to Christmas and trot them out in August.

MORGENHALL. You couldn't share it?

FOWLE. Not to that extent. I often missed the funny point.

MORGENHALL. Then you'd quarrel?

FOWLE. 'Don't look so miserable, it may never happen.' She said that every night when I came home. 'Where'd you get that miserable expression from?'

MORGENHALL. I can see it now. There is a kind of Sunday evening appearance to you.

FOWLE. I was quite happy. But it was always 'Cat got your tongue?' 'Where's the funeral?' 'Play us a tune on that old fiddle face of yours. Lucky there's one of us here that can see the funny side.' Then we had to have our tea with the wireless on, so that she'd pick up the phrases.

MORGENHALL. You're not a wireless lover?

FOWLE. I couldn't always laugh. And she'd be doubled up across the table, gasping as if her lungs were full of water. 'Laugh,' she'd call, 'Laugh, damn you. What've you got to be so miserable about?' Then she'd go under, bubbling like a drowning woman.

MORGENHALL. Made meals difficult?

FOWLE. Indigestible. I would have laughed, but the jokes never tickled me.

MORGENHALL. They tickled her?

FOWLE. Anything did. Anything a little comic. Our names were misfortunate.

MORGENHALL. Your names?

FOWLE. Fowle. Going down the aisle she said: 'Now we're cock and hen, aren't we, old bird?' Coming away, it was 'Now I'm Mrs Fowle, you'll have to play fair with me.' She laughed so hard we couldn't get her straightened up for the photograph.

MORGENHALL. Fond of puns, I gather you're trying to say.

FOWLE. Of any sort of joke. I had a little aviary at the bottom of my garden. As she got funnier so I spent more time with my birds. Budgerigars are small parrots. Circles round their eyes give them a sad, tired look.

MORGENHALL. You found them sympathetic?

FOWLE. Restful. Until one of them spoke out at me.

MORGENHALL. Spoke – what words?

FOWLE. 'Don't look so miserable, it may never happen.'

MORGENHALL. The bird said that?

FOWLE. She taught it during the day when I was out at work. It didn't mean to irritate.

MORGENHALL. It was wrong of her of course. To lead on your bird like that.

FOWLE. But it wasn't him that brought me to it. It was Bateson, the lodger.

MORGENHALL. Another man?

FOWLE. At long last.

MORGENHALL. I can see it now. A crime of passion. An unfaithful wife. *In flagrante* . . . Of course, you don't know what that means. We'll reduce it to manslaughter right away. A wronged husband and there's never a dry eye in the jury-box. You came in and caught them.

FOWLE. Always laughing together.

MORGENHALL. Maddening!

FOWLE. He knew more jokes than she did.

MORGENHALL. Stealing her before your eyes?

FOWLE. That's what I thought. He was a big man. Ex-police. Said he'd been the scream of the station. I picked him for her specially. In the chitty I put up in the local sweet shop, I wrote: 'Humorous type of lodger wanted.'

MORGENHALL. But wasn't that a risk?

FOWLE. Slight, perhaps. But it went all right. Two days after he came he poised a bag of flour to fall on her in the kitchen. Then she sewed up the legs of his pyjamas. They had to hold on to each other so as not to fall over laughing. 'Look at old misery standing there,' she said. 'He can never see anything subtle.'

MORGENHALL. Galling for you. Terribly galling.

FOWLE. I thought all was well. I spent more time with the

birds. I'd come home late and always be careful to scrunch the gravel at the front door. I went to bed early and left them with the Light Programme. On Sunday mornings I fed the budgies and suggested he took her tea in bed. 'Laughter,' she read out from her horoscope, 'leads to love, even for those born under the sign of the Virgin.'

MORGENHALL. You trusted them. They deceived you.

FOWLE. They deceived me all right. And I trusted them. Especially after I'd seen her on his knee and them both looking at the cartoons from one wrapping of chips.

MORGENHALL. Mr Fowle. I'm not quite getting the drift of your evidence. My hope is – your thought may not prove a shade too involved for our literal-minded judge. Old Tommy Banter was a Rugger blue in '98. He never rose to chess and his draughts had a brutal, unintelligent quality.

FOWLE. When he'd first put his knee under her I thought he'd do the decent thing. I thought I'd have peace in my little house at last. The wireless set dead silent. The end of all the happy laughter. No sound but the twitter from the end of the garden and the squeak of my own foot on the linoleum.

MORGENHALL. You wanted . . .

FOWLE. I heard them whispering together and my hopes raised high. Then I came back and he was gone.

MORGENHALL. She'd . . .

FOWLE. Turned him out. Because he was getting over familiar. 'I couldn't have that.' she said. 'I may like my laugh, but thank God, I'm still respectable. No thank you, there's safety in marriage. So I'm stuck with you, fiddle face. Let's play a tune on it, shall we?' She'd sent him away, my last hope.

MORGENHALL. So you . . .

FOWLE. I realize I did wrong.

MORGENHALL. You could have left.

FOWLE. Who'd have fed the birds? That thought was upper-most.

MORGENHALL. So it's not a crime of passion?

FOWLE. Not if you put it like that.

MORGENHALL. Mr Fowle. I've worked and waited for you. Now, you're the only case I've got, *and* the most difficult.

FOWLE. I'm sorry.

MORGENHALL. A man could crack his head against a case like you and still be far from a solution. Can't you see how twelve honest hearts will snap like steel when they learn you ended up your wife because she *wouldn't* leave you?

FOWLE. If she had left, there wouldn't have been the need.

MORGENHALL. There's no doubt about it. As I look at you now, I see you're an unsympathetic figure.

FOWLE. There it is.

MORGENHALL. It'll need a brilliant stroke to save you. An unexpected move – something pulled out of a hat – I've got it. Something really exciting. The surprise witness.

FOWLE. Witness?

MORGENHALL. Picture the scene, Mr Fowle. The Court room silent. The jury about to sink you. The prosecution flushed with victory. And then I rise, my voice a hoarse whisper, exhausted by that long trial. 'My Lord. If your Lordship pleases.'

FOWLE. What are you saying?

MORGENHALL. Do you expect me to do this off the cuff, Fowle, with no sort of rehearsal?

FOWLE. No. . . .

MORGENHALL. Take the stool and co-operate, man. Now, that towel over your head, please, to simulate the dirty grey wig – already you appear anonymous and vaguely alarming.

> MORGENHALL *arranges* FOWLE *on the stool. Drapes the towel over his head.*

Now, my dear Fowle, forget your personality. You're Sir

Tommy Banter, living with a widowed sister in a draughty great morgue on Wimbledon Common. Digestion, bad. Politics, an Independent Moral Conservative. Favourite author, doesn't read. Diversions, snooker in the basement of the morgue, peeping at the lovers on the Common and money being given away on the television. In love with capital punishment, corporal punishment, and a younger brother who is accomplished at embroidery. A small, alarmed man, frightened of the great dog he lives with to give him the air of a country squire. Served with distinction in the Great War at sentencing soldiers to long terms of imprisonment. A man without friends, unexpectedly adored by a great-niece, three years old.

FOWLE. I am?

MORGENHALL. Him.

FOWLE. It feels strange.

MORGENHALL. Now, my Lord. I ask your Lordship's leave to call the surprise witness.

FOWLE. Certainly.

MORGENHALL. What?

FOWLE. Certainly.

MORGENHALL. For Heaven's sake, Fowle, this is like practising bull-fights with a kitten. Here's an irregular application by the defence, something that might twist the trial in the prisoner's favour and prevent you catching the connection at Charing Cross. Your breakfast's like a lead weight on your chest. Your sister, plunging at Spot last night, ripped the cloth. The dog bit your ankle on the way downstairs. No, blind yourself with rage and terrible justice.

FOWLE. No. You can't call the surprise witness.

MORGENHALL. That's better. Oh, my Lord. If your Lordship would listen to me.

FOWLE. Certainly not. You've had your chance. Let's get on with it.

MORGENHALL. My Lord. Justice must not only be done, but

must clearly be seen to be done. No one knows, as yet, what my surprise witness will say. Perhaps he'll say the prisoner is guilty in his black heart as your Lordship thinks. But perhaps, gentlemen of the jury, we have trapped an innocent. If so, shall we deny him the one door through which he might walk to freedom? The public outcry would never die down.

FOWLE (*snatching off the towel and rising angrily to his feet*). Hear, hear!

MORGENHALL. What's that?

FOWLE. The public outcry.

MORGENHALL. Excellent. Now, towel back on. You're the judge.

FOWLE (*as the Judge*). Silence! I'll have all those noisy people put out. Very well. Call the witness. But keep it short.

MORGENHALL. Wonderful. Very good. Now. Deathly silence as the witness walks through the breathless crowds. Let's see the surprise witness. Take the towel off.

FOWLE (*moves from the stool and, standing very straight says*): I swear to tell the truth . . .

MORGENHALL. You've got a real feeling for the Law. A pity you came to it so late in life.

FOWLE. The whole truth.

MORGENHALL. Now, what's your name?

FOWLE (*absent minded*). Herbert Fowle.

MORGENHALL. No, no. You're the witness.

FOWLE. Martin Jones.

MORGENHALL. Excellent. Now, you know Herbert Fowle?

FOWLE. All my life.

MORGENHALL. Always found him respectable?

FOWLE. Very quiet spoken man, and clean living.

MORGENHALL. Where was he when this crime took place?

FOWLE. He was . . .

MORGENHALL. Just a moment. My Lord, will you sharpen a
    pencil and note this down?

FOWLE. You'd dare to say that? To him?

MORGENHALL. Fearlessness, Mr Fowle. The first essential in
    an advocate. Is your Lordship's pencil poised?

FOWLE (*as Judge*). Yes, yes. Get on with it.

MORGENHALL. Where was he?

FOWLE (*as Witness*). In my house.

MORGENHALL. All the evening?

FOWLE. Playing whist. I went to collect him and we left Mrs
    Fowle well and happy. I returned with him and she'd been
    removed to the Country and General.

MORGENHALL. Panic stirs the prosecution benches. The
    prosecutor tries a few fumbling questions. But you stand
    your ground, don't you?

FOWLE. Certainly.

MORGENHALL. My Lord. I demand the prisoner be released.

FOWLE (*as Judge*). Certainly. Can't think what all this fuss has
    been about. Release the prisoner, and reduce all police
    officers in Court to the rank of P.C.

    Pause.

MORGENHALL. Fowle.

FOWLE. Yes, sir.

MORGENHALL. Aren't you going to thank me?

FOWLE. I don't know what I can say.

MORGENHALL. Words don't come easily to you, do they?

FOWLE. Very hard.

MORGENHALL. You could just stand and stammer in a
    touching way and offer me that old gold watch of your
    father's.

FOWLE. But . . .

MORGENHALL. Well, I think we've pulled your chestnuts out
    of the fire. We'll just have to make sure of this fellow Jones.

FOWLE. But . . .

MORGENHALL. Fowle, you're a good simple chap, but there's no need to interrupt my thinking.

FOWLE. I was only reminding you . . .

MORGENHALL. Well, what?

FOWLE. We have no Jones.

MORGENHALL. Carried off in a cold spell? Then we can get his statement in under the Evidence Act.

FOWLE. He never lived. We made him up.

Pause.

MORGENHALL. Fowle.

FOWLE. Yes, sir.

MORGENHALL. It's remarkable a thing, but with no legal training, I think you've put your finger on a fatal weakness in our defence.

FOWLE. I was afraid it might be so.

MORGENHALL. It is so.

FOWLE. Then we'd better just give in.

MORGENHALL. Give in? We do not give in. When my life depends on this case.

FOWLE. I forgot. Then, we must try.

MORGENHALL. Yes. Brain! Brain! Go to work. It'll come to me, you know, in an illuminating flash. Hard relentless brain work. This is the way I go at the crosswords and I never give up. I have it. Bateson!

FOWLE. The lodger?

MORGENHALL. Bateson, the lodger. I never liked him. Under a ruthless cross-examination, you know, he might confess that it was he. Do you see a flash?

FOWLE. You look much happier.

MORGENHALL. I am much happier. And when I begin my ruthless cross-examination. . . .

FOWLE. Would you care to try it?

MORGENHALL. Mr Fowle. You and I are learning to muck in splendidly together over this. Mr Bateson.

FOWLE (*as Bateson, lounging in an imaginary witness box with his hands in his pockets*). Yes. Sir?

MORGENHALL. Perhaps, when you address the Court you'd be good enough to take your hands out of your pockets. Not you Mr Fowle, of course. You became on very friendly terms with the prisoner's wife?

FOWLE. We had one or two good old laughs together.

MORGENHALL. Was the association entirely innocent?

FOWLE. Innocent laughs. Jokes without offence. The cracker or Christmas card variety. No jokes that would have shamed a postcard.

MORGENHALL. And to tell those innocent jokes, did you have to sit very close to Mrs Fowle?

FOWLE. How do you mean?

MORGENHALL. Did you have to sit beneath her?

FOWLE. I don't understand.

MORGENHALL. Did she perch upon your knee?

FOWLE (*horrified intake of breath*).

MORGENHALL. What was that?

FOWLE. Shocked breathing from the jury, sir.

MORGENHALL. Having its effect, eh? Now, Mr Bateson. Will you kindly answer my question.

FOWLE. You're trying to trap me.

MORGENHALL. Not trying, Bateson, succeeding.

FOWLE. Well, she may have rested on my knee. Once or twice.

MORGENHALL. And you loved her, guiltily?

FOWLE. I may have done.

MORGENHALL. And planned to take her away with you?

FOWLE. I did ask her.

MORGENHALL. And when she refused. . . .

FOWLE (*as Judge*). Just a moment. Where's all this leading?

MORGENHALL. Your Lordship asks me! My Lord, it is our case that it was this man, Bateson, enraged by the refusal of the prisoner's wife to follow him, who struck . . . You see where we've got to?

FOWLE. I do.

MORGENHALL. Masterly. I think you'll have to agree with me?

FOWLE. Of course.

MORGENHALL. No flaws in this one?

FOWLE. Not really a flaw, sir. Perhaps a little hitch.

MORGENHALL. A hitch. Go on. Break it down.

FOWLE. No, sir, really. Not after you've been so kind.

MORGENHALL. Never mind. All my life I've stood against the winds of criticism and neglect. My gown may be a little tattered, my cuffs frayed. There may be a hole in my sock for the draughts to get at me. Quite often, on my way to Court, I notice that my left shoe lets in water. I am used to hardship. Speak on, Mr Fowle.

FOWLE. Soon as he left my house, Bateson was stopped by an officer. He'd lifted an alarm clock off me, and the remains of a bottle of port. They booked him straight away.

MORGENHALL. You mean, there wasn't time?

FOWLE. Hardly. Two hours later the next door observed Mrs Fowle at the washing. Then I came home.

MORGENHALL. Fowle. Do you want to help me?

FOWLE. Of course. Haven't I shown it?

MORGENHALL. But you will go on putting all these difficulties in my way.

FOWLE. I knew you'd be upset.

MORGENHALL. Not really. After all, I'm a grown up, even an old, man. At my age one expects little gratitude. There's a cat I feed each day at my lodgings, a waitress in the lunch room here who always gets that sixpence under my plate. In ten, twenty years' time, will they remember me? Oh, I'm not bitter. But a little help, just a very little encouragement. . . .

FOWLE. But you'll win this case. A brilliant mind like yours.

MORGENHALL. Yes. Thank God. It's very brilliant.

FOWLE. And all that training.

MORGENHALL. Years of it. Hard, hard training.

FOWLE. You'll solve it, sir.

Pause.

MORGENHALL. Fowle. Do you know what I've heard Tuppy Morgan say? After all, he's sat here, year in, year out, as long as anyone can remember, in Court, waiting for the Dock Brief himself. Wilfred, he's frequently told me, if they ever give you a brief, old fellow, attack the medical evidence. Remember, the jury's full of rheumatism and arthritis and shocking gastric troubles. They love to see a medical man put through it. Always go for a doctor.

FOWLE (*eagerly*). You'd like to try?

MORGENHALL. Shall we?

FOWLE. I'd enjoy it.

MORGENHALL. Doctor. Did you say the lady died of heart failure?

FOWLE (*as Doctor*). No.

MORGENHALL. Come, Doctor. Don't fence with me. Her heart wasn't normal when you examined her, was it?

FOWLE. She was dead.

MORGENHALL. So it had stopped.

FOWLE. Yes.

MORGENHALL. Then her heart had failed?

FOWLE. Well . . .

MORGENHALL. So she died of heart failure?

FOWLE. But . . .

MORGENHALL. And heart failure might have been brought on by a fit, I say a fit of laughter, at a curiously rich joke on the wireless?

FOWLE. Whew!

FOWLE *claps softly. Pause.*

MORGENHALL. Thank you, Fowle. It was kind but, I thought,

hollow. I don't believe my attack on the doctor was convincing.

FOWLE. Perhaps a bit unlikely. But clever. . . .

MORGENHALL. Too clever. No. We're not going to win this on science, Fowle. Science must be thrown away. As I asked those questions, I saw I wasn't even convincing you of your own innocence. But you respond to emotion, Fowle, as I do, the magic of oratory, the wonderful power of words.

FOWLE. Now you're talking.

MORGENHALL. I'm going to talk.

FOWLE. I wish I could hear some of it. Words as grand as print.

MORGENHALL. A golden tongue. A voice like a lyre to charm you out of hell.

FOWLE. Now you've commenced to wander away from all I've understood.

MORGENHALL. I was drawing on the riches of my classical education which comforts me on buses, waiting at surgeries, or in prison cells. But I shall speak to the jury simply, without classical allusions. I shall say . . .

FOWLE. Yes.

MORGENHALL. I shall say . . .

FOWLE. What?

MORGENHALL. I had it on the tip of my tongue.

FOWLE. Oh.

MORGENHALL. I shan't disappoint you. I shall speak for a day, perhaps two days. At the end I shall say . . .

FOWLE. Yes? Just the closing words.

MORGENHALL. The closing words.

FOWLE. To clinch the argument.

MORGENHALL. Yes. The final, irrefutable argument.

FOWLE. If I could only hear.

MORGENHALL. You shall, Fowle. You shall hear it. In Court. It'll come out in Court, and when I sink back in my seat, trembling, and wipe the real tears off my glasses. . . .

c

FOWLE. The judge's summing up.

MORGENHALL. What will Tommy say?

FOWLE (*as Judge*). Members of the jury . . .

MORGENHALL. Struggling with emotions as well.

FOWLE. I can't add anything to the words of the barrister. Go out and consider your verdict.

MORGENHALL. Have they left the box?

FOWLE. Only a formality.

MORGENHALL. I see. I wonder how long they'll be out.

Pause.

They're out a long time.

FOWLE. Of course, it must seem long to you. The suspense.

MORGENHALL. I hope they won't disagree.

FOWLE. I don't see how they can.

Pause.

MORGENHALL. Fowle.

FOWLE. Yes, sir.

MORGENHALL. Shall we just take a peep into the jury room.

FOWLE. I wish we could.

MORGENHALL. Let's. Let me see, you're the foreman?

FOWLE. I take it we're all agreed, chaps. So let's sit here and have a short smoke.

They sit on the bench together.

MORGENHALL. An excellent idea. The barrister saved him.

FOWLE. That wonderful speech. I had a bit of doubt before I heard the speech.

MORGENHALL. No doubt now, have you?

FOWLE. Certainly not.

They light imaginary pipes.

Care for a fill of mine?

MORGENHALL. Thank you so much. Match?

FOWLE. Here you are.

MORGENHALL. I say, you don't think the poor fellow's in any doubt, do you?

FOWLE. No. He must know he'll get off. After the speech I mean.

MORGENHALL. I mean, I wouldn't like him to be on pins. . . .

FOWLE. Think we ought to go back and reassure him?

They move off the bench.

MORGENHALL. As you wish. Careful that pipe doesn't start a fire in your pocket. (*As Clerk of Court*). Gentlemen of the jury. Have you considered your verdict?

FOWLE. We have.

MORGENHALL. And do you find the prisoner guilty or not guilty?

FOWLE. Not guilty, my Lord.

MORGENHALL. Hooray!

FOWLE (*as Judge*). Now, if there's any sort of Mafeking around, I'll have the Court closed.

MORGENHALL. So I'm surrounded, mobbed. Tuppy Morgan wrings my hand and says it was lucky he left the seat. The judge sends me a letter of congratulation. The journalists dart off to their little telephones. And what now: 'Of course they'd make you a judge but you're probably too busy. . . .' There's a queue of solicitors on the stairs. . . . My old clerk writes on my next brief, a thousand guineas to divorce a duchess. There are questions of new clothes, laying down the port. Oh, Mr Fowle, the change in life you've brought me.

FOWLE. It will be your greatest day.

MORGENHALL. Yes, Mr Fowle. My greatest day.

The bolts shoot back, the door opens slowly.

What's that? I said we weren't to be interrupted. It's

draughty in here with that door open. Close it, there's a good chap, do.

FOWLE. I think, you know, they must want us for the trial.
FOWLE *goes through the door.* MORGENHALL *follows with a dramatic sweep of his gown.*

The Curtain Falls

Scene Two

When the curtain rises again the sky through the windows shows that it is late afternoon. The door is unlocked and MORGENHALL *enters. He is without his wig and gown, more agitated than ever, he speaks to the* WARDER, *off stage.*

MORGENHALL. He's not here at the moment – he's not . . . ?
Oh, I'm so glad. Just out temporarily? With the governor?
Then, I'll wait for him. Poor soul. How's he taking it? You're
not allowed to answer questions? The regulations, I suppose.
Well, you must obey the regulations. I'll just sit down here
and wait for Mr Fowle.

The door closes.

(*He whistles. Whistling stops.*) May it please you, my Lord,
members of the jury. I should have said, may it please you,
my *Lord*, members of the jury. I should have said . . .

He begins to walk up and down.

Members of the jury. Is there one of you who doesn't crave
for peace . . . crave for peace. The silence of an undisturbed
life, the dignity of an existence without dependants . . .
without jokes. Have you never been tempted?
I should have said . . .
Members of the *jury*. You and I are men of the world. If
your Lordship would kindly not interrupt my speech to the
jury. I'm obliged. Members of the jury, before I was so
rudely interrupted.
I might have said . . .
Look at the prisoner, members of the jury. Has he hurt you,
done you the slightest harm? Is he not the mildest of men?

He merely took it upon himself to regulate his domestic affairs. An Englishman's home is his castle. Do any of you feel a primitive urge, members of the jury, to be revenged on this gentle bird fancier. . . .

Members of the jury, I see I'm affecting your emotions but let us consider the weight of the evidence . . . I might have said that!

I might have said . . . (*with distress*) I might have said something. . . .

> *The door opens.* FOWLE *enters. He is smiling to himself, but as soon as he sees* MORGENHALL *he looks serious and solicitous.*

FOWLE. I was hoping you'd find time to drop in, sir. I'm afraid you're upset.

MORGENHALL. No, no, my dear chap. Not at all upset.

FOWLE. The result of the trial's upset you.

MORGENHALL. I feel a little dashed. A little out of sorts.

FOWLE. It was disappointing for you.

MORGENHALL. A touch of disappointment. But there'll be other cases. There may be other cases.

FOWLE. But you'd built such high hopes on this particular one.

MORGENHALL. Well, there it is, Fowle.

FOWLE. It doesn't do to expect too much of a particular thing.

MORGENHALL. You're right, of course.

FOWLE. Year after year I used to look forward keenly to the Feathered Friends Fanciers' Annual Do. Invariably it took the form of a dinner.

MORGENHALL. Your yearly treat?

FOWLE. Exactly. All I had in the enjoyment line. Each year I built high hopes on it. June 13th, I'd say, now there's an evening to look forward to.

MORGENHALL. Something to live for?

FOWLE. In a way. But when it came, you know, it was never up to it. Your collar was always too tight, or the food was inadequate, or someone had a nasty scene with the fancier in the chair. So, on June 14th, I always said to myself: Thank God for a night at home.

MORGENHALL. It came and went and your life didn't change?

FOWLE. No, quite frankly.

MORGENHALL. And this case has left me just as I was before.

FOWLE. Don't say that.

MORGENHALL. Tuppy Morgan's back in his old seat under the window. The judge never congratulated me. No one's rung up to offer me a brief. I thought my old clerk looked coldly at me, and there was a titter in the luncheon room when I ordered my usual roll and tomato soup.

FOWLE. But I . . .

MORGENHALL. And you're not left in a very favourable position.

FOWLE. Don't say that, sir. It's not so bad for me. After all, I had no education.

MORGENHALL. So many years before I could master the Roman Law relating to the ownership of chariots. . . .

FOWLE. Wasted, you think?

MORGENHALL. I feel so.

FOWLE. But without that rich background, would an individual have been able to sway the Court as you did?

MORGENHALL. Sway?

FOWLE. The Court.

MORGENHALL. Did I do that?

FOWLE. It struck me you did.

MORGENHALL. Indeed. . . .

FOWLE. It's turned out masterly.

MORGENHALL. Mr Fowle, you're trying to be kind. When I was a child I played French cricket with an uncle who deliberately allowed the ball to strike his legs. At the age of seven that irked me. At sixty-three I can face the difficulties of accurate batting. . . .

FOWLE. But no, sir. I really mean it. I owe it all to you. Where I am.

MORGENHALL. I'm afraid near the end.

FOWLE. Just commencing.

MORGENHALL. I lost, Mr Fowle. You may not be aware of it. It may not have been hammered home to you yet. But your case is lost.

FOWLE. But there are ways and ways of losing.

MORGENHALL. That's true, of course.

FOWLE. I noticed your artfulness right at the start, when the policeman gave evidence. You pulled out that red handkerchief, slowly and deliberately, like a conjuring trick.

MORGENHALL. And blew?

FOWLE. A sad, terrible trumpet.

MORGENHALL. Unnerved him, I thought.

FOWLE. He never recovered. There was no call to ask questions after that.

MORGENHALL. And then they called that doctor.

FOWLE. You were right not to bother with him.

MORGENHALL. Tactics, you see. We'd decided not to trouble with science.

FOWLE. So we had. And with Bateson . . .

MORGENHALL. No, Fowle. I must beware of your flattery, I think I might have asked Bateson . . .

FOWLE. It wouldn't have made a farthing's difference. A glance told them he was a demon.

MORGENHALL. He stood there, so big and red, with his no tie and dirty collar. I rose up to question him and suddenly it seemed as if there were no reason for us to converse. I remembered what you said about his jokes, his familiarity with your wife. What had he and I in common? I turned from him in disgust. I think that jury guessed the reason for my silence with friend Bateson.

FOWLE. I think they did!

MORGENHALL. But when it came to the speech. . . .

FOWLE. The best stroke of all.

MORGENHALL. I can't agree. You no longer carry me with you.

FOWLE. Said from the heart.

MORGENHALL. I'm sure of it. But not, dare I say, altogether justified? We can't pretend, can we, Mr Fowle, that the speech was a success?

FOWLE. It won the day.

MORGENHALL. I beg you not to be under any illusions. They found you guilty.

FOWLE. I was forgetting. But that masterly speech. . . .

MORGENHALL. I can't be hoodwinked.

FOWLE. But you don't know. . . .

MORGENHALL. I stood up, Mr Fowle, and it was the moment I'd waited for. Ambition had driven me to it, the moment when I was alone with what I wanted. Everyone turned to me, twelve blank faces in the jury box, eager to have the grumpy looks wiped off them. The judge was silent. The prosecutor courteously pretended to be asleep. I only had to open my mouth and pour words out. What stopped me?

FOWLE. What?

MORGENHALL. Fear. That's what's suggested. That's what the clerks tittered to the waitress in Friday's luncheon room. Old Wilf Morgenhall was in a funk.

FOWLE. More shame on them. . . .

MORGENHALL. But it wasn't so. Nor did my mind go blank. When I rose I knew exactly what I was going to say.

FOWLE. Then, why?

MORGENHALL. Not say it – you were going to say?

FOWLE. It had struck me –

MORGENHALL. It must have, Fowle. It must have struck many people. You'll forgive a reminiscence. . . .

FOWLE. Glad of one.

MORGENHALL. The lady I happened to mention yesterday. I
don't of course, often speak of her. . . .

FOWLE. She, who, in the 1914 . . . ?

MORGENHALL. Exactly. But I lost her long before that. For
years, you know, Mr Fowle, this particular lady and I met
at tea parties, tennis, and so on. Then, one evening, I walked
home with her. We stood on Vauxhall Bridge, a warm
Summer night, and silence fell. It was the moment when I
should have spoken, the obvious moment. Then, something
overcame me, it wasn't shyness or fear then, but a
tremendous exhaustion. I was tired out by the long wait,
and when the opportunity came – all I could think of was
sleep.

FOWLE. It's a relief. . . .

MORGENHALL. To go home alone. To undress, clean your
teeth, knock out your pipe, not to bother with failure or
success.

FOWLE. So yesterday . . .

MORGENHALL. I had lived through that moment so many
times. It happened every day in my mind, daydreaming on
buses, or in the doctor's surgery. When it came, I was tired
of it. The exhaustion came over me. I wanted it to be all
over. I wanted to be alone in my room, in the darkness, with
a soft pillow round my ears. . . . So I failed.

FOWLE. Don't say it.

MORGENHALL. Being too tired to make my daydream public.
It's a nice day. Summer's coming.

FOWLE. No, don't sir. Not too near the window.

MORGENHALL. Why not, Mr Fowle?

FOWLE. I was concerned. A man in your position might be
desperate. . . .

MORGENHALL. You say you can see the forest?

FOWLE. Just a glimpse of it.

MORGENHALL. I think I shall retire from the bar.

FOWLE. Don't say it, sir. After that rigorous training.

MORGENHALL. Well, there it is. I think I shall retire.

FOWLE. But cheer up, sir. As you said, other cases, other days. Let's take this calmly, sir. Let's be very lucid, as you put it in your own statement.

MORGENHALL. Other cases? I'm getting on, you know. Tuppy Morgan's back in his place. I doubt if the Dock Brief will come round again.

FOWLE. But there'll be something.

MORGENHALL. What can there be? Unless?

FOWLE. Yes, sir?

MORGENHALL. There would be another brief if . . .

FOWLE. Yes?

MORGENHALL. I advised you to appeal. . . .

FOWLE. Ah, now that, misfortunately . . .

MORGENHALL. There's a different atmosphere there, up in the Appeal Court, Fowle. It's far from the rough and tumble, question and answer, swear on the Bible and lie your way out of it. It's quiet up there. Pure Law, of course. Yes. I believe I'm cut out for the Court of Appeal. . . .

FOWLE. But you see . . .

MORGENHALL. A big, quiet Court in the early Summer afternoon. Piles of books, and when you put one down the dust and powdered leather rises and makes the ushers sneeze. The clock ticks. Three old judges in scarlet take snuff with trembling hands. You'll sit in the dock and not follow a legal word. And I'll give them all my Law and get you off on a technicality.

FOWLE. But today . . .

MORGENHALL. Now, if I may remind your Lordships of Prickle against the Haverfordwest Justice *ex parte* Anger, reported in 96 Moor's Ecclesiastical at page a thousand and three. Have your Lordships the report? Lord Bradwell, C. J., says, at the foot of the page: 'The guilty intention is a deep foundation stone in the wall of our jurisprudence. So if

it be that Prickle did run the bailiff through with his
poignard taking him for a stray dog or cat, it seems there
would be well raised the plea of autrefois mistake. But,
contra, if he thought him to be his neighbour's cat, then, as
my Brother Breadwinkle has well said in Lord Roche and
Anderson, there might fall out a constructive larceny and
felo in rem.' Oh, Mr Fowle, I have some of these fine cases
by heart.

FOWLE. Above me, I'm afraid, you're going now.

MORGENHALL. Of course I am. These cases always bore the
prisoner until they're upheld or overruled and he comes out
dead or alive at the end of it all.

FOWLE. I'd like to hear you reading them, though. . . .

MORGENHALL. You will. I'll be followed to Court by my
clerk, an old tortoise burdened by the weight of authorities.
Then he'll lay them out in a fine buff and half calf row, a
letter from a clergyman I correspond with in Wales torn to
mark each place. A glass of water, a dry cough and the 'My
respectful submission'.

FOWLE. And that, of course, is . . .

MORGENHALL. That the judge misdirected himself. He
forgot the rule in Rimmer's case, he confused his *mens sana,*
he displaced the burden of proof, he played fast and loose
with all reasonable doubt, he kicked the presumption of
innocence round like a football.

FOWLE. Strong words.

MORGENHALL. I shan't let Tommy Banter off lightly.

FOWLE. The judge?

MORGENHALL. Thoroughly unscholarly. Not a word of
Latin in the whole summing up.

FOWLE. Not up to you, of course.

MORGENHALL. Thank God, I kept my books. There have
been times, Fowle, when I was tempted, pricked and harried
for rent perhaps, to have my clerk barter the whole lot away
for the few pounds they offer for centuries of entombed law.

But I stuck to them. I still have my Swabey and Tristram, my Pod's *Privy Council*, my Spinks' *Prize Cases*. I shall open them up and say . . . I shall say . . .

FOWLE. It's no good.

MORGENHALL. What's no good?

FOWLE. It's no good appealing.

MORGENHALL. No good?

FOWLE. No good at all.

MORGENHALL. Mr Fowle. I've worked hard for you.

FOWLE. True enough.

MORGENHALL. And I mean to go on working.

FOWLE. It's a great comfort . . .

MORGENHALL. In the course of our close, and may I say it? yes, our happy collaboration on this little crime of yours, I've become almost fond of you.

FOWLE. Thank you, sir.

MORGENHALL. At first, I have to admit it, I was put off by your somewhat furtive and repulsive appearance. I saw, I quite agree, only the outer husk, and what I saw was a small man marked by all the physical signs of confirmed criminality.

FOWLE. No oil painting?

MORGENHALL. Let's agree on that at once.

FOWLE. The wife thought so, too.

MORGENHALL. Enough of her, poor woman.

FOWLE. Oh, agreed.

MORGENHALL. My first solicitude for your well-being, let's face up to this as well, had a selfish element. You were my very own case, and I didn't want to lose you.

FOWLE. Natural feelings. But still . . .

MORGENHALL. I haven't wounded you?

FOWLE. Nothing fatal.

MORGENHALL. I'm glad. Because, you know, as we worked on this case together, an affection sprang up . . .

FOWLE. Mutual.

MORGENHALL. You seemed to have a real desire to help, and, if I may say so, an instinctive taste for the law.

FOWLE. A man can't go through this sort of thing without getting legal interests.

MORGENHALL. Quite so. And of course, as a self-made man, that's to your credit. But I did notice, just at the start, some flaws in you as a client.

FOWLE. Flaws?

MORGENHALL. You may not care to admit it. But let's be honest. After all, we don't want to look on the dreary side; but you may not be with us for very long. . . .

FOWLE. That's what I was trying to say. . . .

MORGENHALL. Please, Mr Fowle, no interruptions until we've cleared this out of the way. Now didn't you, just at the beginning, put unnecessary difficulties before us?

FOWLE. Did I?

MORGENHALL. I well remember, before I got a bit of keenness into you, that you seemed about to admit your guilt.

FOWLE. Oh. . . .

MORGENHALL. Just a little obstinate, wasn't it?

FOWLE. I dare say. . . .

MORGENHALL. And now, when I've worked for fifty years to get the Law at my finger-tips, I hear you mutter, 'No appeal'.

FOWLE. No appeal!

MORGENHALL. Mr Fowle. . . .

FOWLE. Yesterday you asked me to spare you pain, sir. This is going to be very hard for me.

MORGENHALL. What?

FOWLE. As you say, we've worked together, and I've had the pleasure of watching the ticking over of a legal mind. If you'd call any afternoon I'd be pleased to repay the compliment by showing you my birds. . . .

MORGENHALL. Not in this world you must realize, unless we appeal.

FOWLE. You see, this morning I saw the Governor.

MORGENHALL. You had some complaint?

FOWLE. I don't want to boast, but the truth is . . . he sent for me.

MORGENHALL. You went in fear . . .

FOWLE. And trembling. But he turned out a very gentlemanly sort of individual. Ex-Army, I should imagine. All the ornaments of a gentleman. Wife and children in a tinted photo framed on the desk, handsome oil painting of a prize pig over the mantelpiece. Healthy red face. Strong smell of scented soap. . . .

MORGENHALL. But grow to the point. . . .

FOWLE. I'm telling you. 'Well, Fowle' he says, 'Sit down do. I'm just finishing this letter.' So I sat and looked out of his windows. Big wide windows in the Governor's office, and the view. . . .

MORGENHALL. Fowle. If this anecdote has any point, be a good little chap, reach it.

FOWLE. Of course it has, where was I?

MORGENHALL. Admiring the view as usual.

FOWLE. Panoramic it was. Well, this Governor individual, finishing his letter, lit up one of those flat type of Egyptian cigarettes. 'Well, Fowle,' he said . . .

MORGENHALL. Yes, yes. It's not necessary, Fowle, to reproduce every word of this conversation. Give us the gist, just the meat, you understand. Leave out the trimmings.

FOWLE. Trimmings there weren't. He put it quite bluntly.

MORGENHALL. What did he put?

FOWLE. 'Well, Fowle, this may surprise you. But the Home Office was on the telephone about you this morning.' Isn't that a Government department?

MORGENHALL. Yes, yes, and well . . .

FOWLE. It seems they do, in his words, come through from time to time, and just on business, of course, on that blower. And quite frankly, he admitted he was as shocked as I was. But the drill is, as he phrased it, a reprieve.

MORGENHALL. A . . . ?

FOWLE. It's all over. I'm free. It seems that trial was no good at all. . . .

MORGENHALL. No good. But why?

FOWLE. Oh, no particular reason.

MORGENHALL. There must be a reason. Nothing passes in the Law without a reason.

FOWLE. You won't care to know.

MORGENHALL. Tell me.

FOWLE. You're too busy to wait. . . .

MORGENHALL. Tell me, Mr Fowle. I beg of you. Tell me directly why this Governor, who knows nothing of the Law, should have called our one and only trial together 'No good'.

FOWLE. You yourself taught me not to scatter information like bombs.

MORGENHALL. Mr Fowle. You must answer my question. My legal career may depend on it. If I'm not to have wasted my life on useless trials.

FOWLE. You want to hear?

MORGENHALL. Certainly.

FOWLE. He may not have been serious. There was a twinkle, most likely, in his eye.

MORGENHALL. But he said . . .

FOWLE. That the barrister they chose for me was no good. An old crock, in his words. No good at all. That he never said a word in my defence. So my case never got to the jury. He said the whole business was ever so null and void, but I'd better be careful in the future. . . .

MORGENHALL *runs across the cell, mounts the stool, begins to undo his tie.*

No! Mr Morgenhall! Come down from there! No, sir! Don't do it.

They struggle. FOWLE *brings Morgenhall to earth.*

Don't you see? If I'd had a barrister who asked questions,

and made clever speeches I'd be as dead as mutton. Your
artfulness saved me. . . .

MORGENHALL. My . . .

FOWLE. The artful way you handled it. The dumb tactics.
They paid off! I'm alive!

MORGENHALL. There is that. . . .

FOWLE. And so are you.

MORGENHALL. We both are?

FOWLE. I'm free.

MORGENHALL. To go back to your birds. I suppose . . .

FOWLE. Yes, Mr Morgenhall?

MORGENHALL. It's unlikely you'll marry again?

FOWLE. Unlikely.

Long pause.

MORGENHALL. But you have the clear appearance of a
criminal. I suppose it's not impossible that you might
commit some rather more trivial offence.

FOWLE. A man can't live, Mr Morgenhall, without committing
some trivial offences. Almost daily.

MORGENHALL. Then we may meet again. You may need my
services. . . .

FOWLE. Constantly.

MORGENHALL. The future may not be so black. . . .

FOWLE. The sun's shining.

MORGENHALL. Can we go?

FOWLE. I think the door's been open some time. (*He tries it.
It is unbolted and swings open.*) After you, Mr Morgenhall,
please.

MORGENHALL. No, no.

FOWLE. A man of your education should go first.

MORGENHALL. I think you should lead the way, Mr Fowle,
and as your legal adviser I will follow at a discreet distance,
to straighten out such little tangles as you may hope to
leave in your wake. Let's go.

D

MORGENHALL : *whistles his fragment of tune.* FOWLE : *his whistle joins* MORGENHALL'S. *Whistling they leave the cell,* MORGENHALL *executing, as he leaves, the steps of a small delighted dance.*

Slow Curtain

What Shall We Tell Caroline?

Michael Codron with David Hall (for Talbot Productions Ltd.) presented *What Shall We Tell Caroline?* in a double bill (with *The Dock Brief*) at the Lyric Opera House, Hammersmith, on April 9, 1958, and on May 20, 1958 at the Garrick Theatre. The cast was as follows:

LILY LOUDON ('BIN')	*Brenda Bruce*
ARTHUR LOUDON	*Maurice Denham*
TONY PETERS	*Michael Hordern*
CAROLINE	*Marianne Benet*

Directed by Stuart Burge
Designed by Disley Jones

Scene One

The LOUDON'S *living room at 'Highland Close School', Coldsands. It is an extremely dilapidated room given an air of festivity, as the curtain rises, by the fact that a table is set for four and there are candles in odd candlesticks – one expensive silver, the other a china 'Present from Coldsands' on the table. Doors on each side of the room, one, left, is covered in green baize and has pinned on it a few yellowing curling notices and charts of lessons which haven't been read for years. The door is closed and leads to the boys' part of the house. The door on the right is open and light floods through it from a staircase which leads to the bedrooms. Another door backstage right leads to the kitchen. At the back of the room tall French windows, which have never shut properly and let in winds of icy severity, open on to a strip of grey asphalt, the white end of a flag pole and the gun-metal sky of an early evening in March.*

Other furniture : a basket-work chair, a fireplace full of paper, a very small electric fire, a horse-hair sofa wounded and bleeding its stuffing ; a roll top desk out of which bills, writs, exercise books and reports are perpetually being shaken by the draughts like the leaves of a dead tree. On top of the desk there is a ukelele and a globe. Among faded photographs of various teams an oar is hanging on the wall.

As the curtain rises LILY LOUDON *has her back to the audience and is tugging at one of the drawers. As she tugs the drawer comes right out and the globe falls down with a sickening crash.*

The crash is immediately followed by a roar from the lit door which leads to the bedrooms. It is the voice of a small man entirely consumed with rage.

ARTHUR (*off*). Imbecile!

LILY *picks up the globe with great calmness and puts it back on the desk, thoughtfully spinning it to find England.*

(*Off.*) Lunatic! Fool! Whatever have you ruined now! What's broken! Go on. Don't keep it from me! Confess!

LILY *picks up the drawer and carries it towards the table. She is an untidy woman, once inconspicuously good looking, whose face now wears an expression of puzzled contentment. She is wearing a lace evening dress of the late thirties, a number of straps are showing on her pale shoulders and a cigarette is dangling from a corner of her mouth. She shows no reaction at all to the diatribe from off stage.*

ARTHUR (*off*). Just try and picture me. Stuck up here. Listening, always listening while you systematically destroy. . . .

LILY *puts the drawer down on the table and knocks off a glass.*

(*Off.*) Aaah. What was that? The last of my dead mother's crockery? Speak up. Put me out of my agony. For pity's sake . . . The suspense. . . . What was it you imbecile? Side plate – dinner plate – not . . .? You're not to be trusted on your own. . . .

LILY *takes out a number of presents wrapped in bright paper and tied with ribbon and arranges them on the table. . . .*

(*Off.*) Where are they? You've hidden them again?

LILY *smiles to herself. Carefully puts out her cigarette.*

(*Off.*) Do you realize what the time is?

LILY *shakes her head.*

ARTHUR (*off*). Dusk. Have you done it? Answer me, can't you? The loneliness – of getting dressed.

LILY *puts a parcel by the place laid in the centre of the table.* ARTHUR *erupts into the room. He is a small, bristly, furiously angry man. He is wearing the trousers only of a merciless tweed suit, no collar and his braces are hanging down his back.*

(*His anger becoming plaintive.*) You can't imagine what a fly you are in the ointment of any little ceremony like this. . . . How you take the edge off my pleasure in any small moment of celebration. My own daughter's birthday. A thing I've been keenly looking forward to and you deliberately . . . hide . . . my . . . clothes.

> LILY *puts the drawer, empty now, back in the desk and comes back to face her husband.*

Perhaps it's a mental kink in you. Is that the excuse you'd make? Do you plead insanity? If I had a pound for every time you've taken a collar stud and . . . I don't know – eaten it . . . rolled it under the chest of drawers. Now, to carefully conceal the club braces. . . . The sort of kink that makes women pinch things in Woolworths. Itching, destructive fingers. Furtive little pickers.

> LILY *pulls his braces, which are hanging down the back of his trousers up across his shoulders, and fastens them. Then she kisses his forehead. This quietens him for a moment. Then he bursts out again.*

That's hardly the point. It's dusk.

> *He runs to the windows and throws them open. A wind, howling in, makes the candles flicker.* ARTHUR *is hauling down the flag.*

LILY. It's bitterly cold.
ARTHUR. Found your tongue at last?
LILY. I said, it's bitterly cold.
ARTHUR (*comes back into the room, the Union Jack bundled in his arms. He kicks the windows shut behind him*). Of course it's

bitterly cold. That wind's come a long way. All the way from the Ural mountains. An uninterrupted journey.

LILY. Yes, I know.

ARTHUR (*folding up the flags – calm for the moment*). Think of that. From Moscow and Vitebsk. The marshes of Poland. The flats of Prussia. The dykes of Belgium and Holland. All the way to Yarmouth. Just think of it. Flat as a playground. That's what I tell the boys.

LILY. I know you do.

ARTHUR. It's a geographical miracle. It makes this place so ideal for schooling boys. There's nothing like a wind from the Ural Mountains, Bin, for keeping boys pure in heart.

LILY. I suppose not.

ARTHUR. Added to which it kills bugs.

LILY. Yes, of course.

ARTHUR. Bugs and unsuitable thoughts. You know that, Bin. You're in charge of that side of it. Have we had a single epidemic this year?

LILY. They cough in the night time. (*She is arranging the presents on the table.*) Like sheep.

ARTHUR. Colds admitted. Infectious diseases not. I had a letter only the other day. A school in Torquay. Malaria. Decimated the boys. Brought on by the relaxing climate. Thank heavens, Bin, for our exposed position.

LILY. Yes, dear.

ARTHUR. For heaven's sake don't complain about the wind, then. It gets on the nerves of a saint. To have you always carping at the wind. Think of it – one little mountain range between here and Moscow and the boys might all go down with malaria.

LILY. I wonder if Caroline's going to like her presents?

ARTHUR. Like her presents? Of course she's going to like her presents. Doesn't she always like her presents?

LILY. I only wondered. . . .

ARTHUR. If you set out to make her dissatisfied. If you sow

the seeds of doubt in her young mind. . . . If you deliberately
undertake to puzzle and bewilder a young girl with your
extraordinary ideas of what a present *ought* to be. If you carp
and criticize. . . .

LILY. I only wondered . . . if she wasn't getting on a bit for
Halma.

ARTHUR. You wondered? Caroline takes it for granted.
Every year she'll get her Halma and every year you'll lose
three or four of her men. . . . Swallow them up like collar
studs. Of course she likes Halma, you've seen her in the
evenings playing it with . . .

*He puts the folded flag on top of the desk. Then shouts as he
picks up the ukulele.*

ARTHUR. He was here again last night!

LILY. Who?

ARTHUR. Tony Peters.

LILY. He's been here for eighteen years.

ARTHUR. But this wasn't here yesterday. He's been lurking
about when I didn't know. *Singing* to you.

LILY *smiles complacently downwards.* ARTHUR *shouts and
holds out the ukulele. She takes it and holds it as if to play it.
She stands still in the attitude of someone about to play the
ukulele during the ensuing dialogue. The French windows open
and* TONY PETERS *enters. He is tall, debonair, and gay,
although balding, with the cuffs of his blazer slightly fraying,
his suede shoes shiny and his grey flannel trousers faded.
He is carrying a string bag full of screw top bottles of light
ale.*

TONY. It's bloody cold.

ARTHUR. It's you.

TONY. Of course it's me. Look here, old man. Aren't you going
to dress? I mean it is Caroline's birthday.

ARTHUR. Oh my God. How far can I be goaded?

TONY (*unloads his bag, sets the bottles out on the table and then throws it on top of the Union Jack.*) I don't know. It's amusing to find out.

ARTHUR. You were here last night?

TONY. Certainly.

ARTHUR. Singing to Bin?

TONY. Keeping her company while you gave. to those few unlucky boys whose temperatures are still normal and who can still breathe through their noses, your usual Sunday evening sermon on 'Life as a stiff row from Putney to Mortlake'.

ARTHUR. So you chose that as a moment for singing . . . to a married woman.

TONY. She sat in your chair, Arthur. We turned out the lights. The room was softly lit by the one bar of the electric fire. I was cross-legged on the floor. In the half-light I appeared boyish and irresistible. Lily needs no concealed lighting to look perpetually young. From under all the doors and through the cracks of the windows the wind sneered at us from Moscow – but we didn't feel the cold. In the distance we heard you say that it is particularly under Hammersmith Bridge that God requires ten hard pulls on the oar. Above us the coughs crackled like distant gunfire. My fingers cramped by the cold, I struck at my instrument. (*He takes the ukulele from* LILY *and plays.*)

(*Singing*)   'Oh the Captain's name
              Was Captain Brown,
              And he played his ukulele
              As the ship went down. . . .'

ARTHUR. That idiotic song.

TONY (*singing very close to Arthur*).
              'Then he bought himself
              A bar of soap,
              And washed himself
              Ashore.'

LILY *puts her hand flat over her mouth like a child to stifle her giggles.*

ARTHUR. If either of you had the slightest idea of loyalty. If you had a grain of respect for me, for Sunday evening, for decent, wholesome living.

TONY (*singing*).

'Oh we left her baby on the shore,
A thing that we've never done before.'

ARTHUR. It's obscene.

TONY. Obscene?

ARTHUR. Perhaps not the words. The dirty expression you put into it. When I'm not looking.

TONY (*singing*).   'If you see the mother
Tell her gently
That we left her baby on the shore.'

The giggles explode past LILY'S *hand.*

ARTHUR. Bin!

LILY. I'm sorry. It just gets me every time. Poor baby! It's so damned casual.

ARTHUR. It doesn't seem to me a subject for joking.

LILY. But the way Tony sings it. Just as if he'd forgotten a baby.

ARTHUR. He probably has.

LILY. What can you be saying?

ARTHUR. I don't know. How can I know anything? Everything goes on when I'm not there. Furniture falls to the ground. This man sings. Crockery breaks. You pull his ears, stroke his hair as he squats there in front of you. Don't think I've got no imagination. I've got a vivid imagination. And my hearing is keen. Remember that. I warn you both. My hearing is exceptionally keen.

TONY. Hear that Lily? Stroke my hair more quietly in future.

As ARTHUR *seems about to hit him a clock groans and strikes off stage.*

LILY. Arthur. You must get dressed. It's nearly time. Caroline'll be down.

ARTHUR. Let her come down. It's time she found out something. Let her find out the lying and deceit and infidelity that all these years . . . let her find out that her mother spends musical evenings breathing down the neck of an ex-night club gigolo, lounge lizard, wallflower, sensitive plant, clinging vine, baby leaving, guitar twanging, Mayfair playboy, good-time Charlie, fly-by-night, moonlight flit, who can't even do quadratic equations. Let her find out all she is. Poor girl. Poor child. You're right Bin – you've brought it on us all. She's too old for Halma now.

He sits down exhausted. They look at him in horror. He, too, is a little horrified by what he has said.

TONY. Arthur. Look here, my dear old fellow. It's Caroline's party. You wouldn't spoil a party?

ARTHUR. I don't know that I feel particularly festive.

LILY. Come on, Arthur. You know how you enjoy Caroline's birthday.

ARTHUR. I always have. Up to now. Ever since she was born.

TONY. And look Arthur, my dear old Head, I bought these for us in the pub. A whiff each after dinner.

He takes two battered cigars out of his breast pocket.

ARTHUR (*crackles and smells the cigar*). That was thoughtful of you, Peters.

TONY. I know you don't smoke them as often as one might like. Only when something a little bit festive arises from time to time.

LILY (*ecstatic*). Oh, Tony Peters! Beautifully managed.

ARTHUR. Perhaps my suspicions are unfounded.

LILY. You manage him so beautifully.

TONY. Why not finish dressing, my fine old headmaster? Let us both face the fact, you must be bitterly cold.

ARTHUR (*starts to work himself up again*). I tell you I never feel cold. Anyway it's never cold here. Only occasionally a little brisk after sunset. Anyway who's old? Didn't you tell me, Tony Peters, that in your prep school the Third Eleven Match play was once stopped by a Zeppelin? You didn't mean to let that slide out did you? What does that make you? Pretty long in bottle for a junior assistant! Ha! Ha!

TONY. I'm not a junior assistant.

ARTHUR. What are you then?

TONY. A senior assistant.

ARTHUR. You're the only assistant. I think of you as junior.

TONY (*shrugging his shoulders*). It's a fact. I give an impression of perpetual youth. (*He slaps his pocket, brings out a half-bottle of whisky.*) I thought this might slip down well with the whiffs.

ARTHUR (*mollified*). It looks like good stuff.

TONY. I've always had an eye for a piece of good stuff.

ARTHUR *looks up suspiciously.*

TONY. Arthur, Head, do believe me. That remark was in no way meant to be offensive.

ARTHUR. I'll take your word for it.

LILY. So hurry on Arthur do. We must be just so for when Caroline comes in.

TONY. Go on Head. Spick and span. That's the order of the day. Look, Lily's in her best. As always, on these occasions.

LILY *and* TONY *pat him, steer him towards the door; he turns to them before he goes out.*

ARTHUR. For God's sake, you two. Use your imaginations. Think what it's like being up there, wrestling with a collar in utter ignorance. Tormented. . . .

TONY. Get a start on the collar now. You'll be back with us in five minutes.

ARTHUR. Five minutes? Haven't you ever thought, Peters, the whole course of a man's life can be changed in five minutes. Does it take five minutes to die? Or catch malaria? Or say the one word to unhinge another man's wife from him? All right, I'll trust you. But look here, both. No singing. Don't torture me with that.

TONY. If I do sing, I'll sing so quietly that no human ear could ever pick it up. I'll sing in notes only audible to a dog.

ARTHUR. That's worse.

LILY. Now go on, really. Caroline can't sit and gaze at a brass collar stud on her birthday.

ARTHUR. I'm going. For Caroline's sake, I'm going. Poor child. (*He stands in the doorway, the door open.*)

TONY. For Caroline's sake. Goodbye.

> TONY *shuts the door on him. Then walks over to the basketwork chair and drops into it.*

TONY. He's not right.

LILY. About what?

TONY. About me.

LILY. What about you?

TONY. I *can* do quadratic equations.

LILY. Another year gone. Another birthday come again.

TONY. Gather all the Xs and Ys on to one side.

LILY. Eighteen years old. (*She fiddles with the presents.*)

TONY. Remove the brackets.

LILY. Oh Tony, can she possibly be happy?

TONY. Remember that minus times minus makes plus.

LILY. Tony can you hear me?

TONY. As an example. In the problem, if it takes ten barbers twenty minutes at double speed to shave 'y' tramps let 'x' equal the time taken to shave half a tramp. That's Arthur's problem. Arthur can *teach* quadratics all right. But can he *do* them. Isn't that rather the point?

LILY. Everyone here is so taken up with their own concerns.

TONY. I'm sorry.

LILY. I quite understand. You're naturally anxious for your algebra.

TONY. No, Lily. Not at all. Come and sit down.

LILY. Where?

TONY. Here. (*He slaps his knee.*)

LILY. I'd be taking a risk.

TONY. All we can take in this mean, tight-fisted world.

> *She giggles and sits on the floor in front of him, her elbows on his knees, gazing up at him.*

LILY. Now is Caroline . . .?

TONY. What?

LILY. Happy.

TONY. She shows no signs of being otherwise.

LILY (*looks down suddenly. Her eyes full of tears*). How can she tell us?

TONY. Poor Arthur. It may not be so bad as he thinks.

LILY. When it's something we must have all noticed why don't we discuss. . . .

TONY. At first perhaps, it was our headmaster's fault. When it happened at first I blamed him. But since last birthday I've begun to suspect. . . .

LILY. Tony. You're talking about it. About Caroline. . . .

TONY (*talking quickly as if to avoid an awkward moment*). Caroline is now eighteen which must mean that she was born in 1940. Dark days with storm clouds hanging over Europe. Poor child she never knew the pre-war when you could week-end in Paris on a two-pound ten note and get a reasonable packet of cigarettes for elevenpence complete with card which could be collected towards a jolly acceptable free gift. She never borrowed a bus and took a couple of girls from

Elstree Studio out dancing up the Great West Road and home with the milk and change left out of a pound.

LILY *begins to smile up at him.*

LILY. It's yourself you're discussing.

TONY. She missed the Big Apple and the Lambeth Walk and the Palais Glide. She couldn't even come to the party I gave for the Jubilee. Poor child, God knows I'd have invited her. Twenty-three of us in a line gliding down the Earls Court Road at three in the morning. Smooth as skaters. (*Takes up his ukelele and sings.*)

> 'She was sweet sixteen.
> On the village green.
> Poor little Angeline.'

ARTHUR (*off stage shouting*). For pity's sake.

TONY *shrugs his shoulders and puts his ukelele down, exasperated.*

TONY. Really. He's like my old landlady in the Earls Court Road. Bump on the ceiling with a broom if you so much as lifted a girl from the floor to the sofa.

LILY (*elbows on his knees*). Was it so carefree for you then, in Earls Court?

TONY (*modestly*). Carefree? Look Lily, I knew ten clubs where the drummers were happy to allow me a whirl with their sticks. I knew twenty pubs in S.W. alone which were flattered to take my cheque, and as for the opposite sex. . . .

LILY *looks at him admiringly.*

I had enough telephone numbers to fill a reasonably bulky pocket diary from January to Christmas. Even the little space for my weight and size of hat, Lily, was crammed with those available numbers.

LILY. What do you think took away all our happy days?

TONY. Are they gone?

LILY. Arthur says so. Driven away, he says, by the Russians and the Socialists and the shocking way they've put up the rates.

TONY. We can still have a good time.

LILY. But can Caroline? If she could only tell. . . .

She gets up and wanders to the table, arranging the presents.

TONY. Well there . . .

LILY. And when she never knew. . . .

TONY. Isn't that rather the point?

LILY. Deprived, Tony, of all the pre-war we ever had?

TONY. All that pre-war denied her.

LILY. What would become of us, do you suppose, if we hadn't got that pre-war to think about?

TONY (*he gets up from the chair and stands with his arm round her shoulders*). It's not all over. We don't just let it die out.

LILY. It mustn't.

TONY. We keep it going you see. And it keeps us going too.

Pause, as they stand side by side.

ARTHUR (*yelling from off stage*). What have you two got to be so damned *quiet* about?

They smile at each other and TONY *breaks away from her and walks round the room rubbing his hands and flapping his arms. He begins to talk in the clipped, stoical voice of an explorer reminiscing.*

TONY. The glass stood at forty below when we unpacked our Christmas dinner in Camp A. (*He blows on his nails.*)

LILY (*thoughtfully, softly*). I remember the day you arrived. It was summer and Arthur was out taking Cricket practice.

TONY. Frozen penguin and a mince pie which my dear sister had sent from Godalming, found, quite by chance, stuffed in a corner of my flea-bag.

E

LILY. I heard the sound of your two-seater on the gravel.

TONY. We broke the mince pie with our ice axes. Three dogs died in the night.

LILY. Why did you have to sell that two-seater?

TONY. . . . Prayed to God before sharing our penguin. Now a thousand miles from base camp. Had a premonition we should never see England again. . . .

LILY. I was alone in the middle of the afternoon. I heard you singing outside the window. It opened and you came in. . . . When you saw me standing all alone. . . .

TONY. Peters . . .

LILY. Yes?

TONY. With silent heroism . . .

LILY. What?

TONY. Walked out of the tent.

With a dramatic gesture he steps behind the curtain of the French window and is lost to sight.

LILY (*standing alone centre stage, her arms extended. A slight wait*). Tony! Why won't you ever be serious with me?

ARTHUR *enters, fully dressed, his hair brushed and shining.*

ARTHUR. Where the hell's he got to now?

LILY *makes a gesture of despair.*

ARTHUR. It's no use lying, Bin. I can see his filthy suede shoes under the curtain.

He pulls the curtain aside. TONY *smiles at him, pats his shoulder and walks out into the room.* TONY *lights a cigarette with great finesse.* ARTHUR *sits down at the table, raises his hands as if to say something several times. The words don't exist for what he feels that he must say.*

TONY. Now Arthur. Don't make a fool of yourself over this

ARTHUR. I . . . make a fool?

TONY. It's quite reasonable.

LILY. Tony, it seems, was discovering the North Pole.

ARTHUR. The North Pole?

TONY. Shut your eyes, Headmaster, and what can you hear? The ice cracking like gun fire in the distance. The wind howling in the guy ropes. The fizz of the solid fuel as it melts a little snow for your evening cocoa.

ARTHUR. Oh my God! (*He buries his face in his hands.*)

LILY (*laughing*). Give the poor man a little peace.

TONY. Peace? What does Arthur want with peace? He'd be as bored as a retired General with nothing to do but keep chickens and explore the possibility of life after death. As lonely as a bull without a bull fighter. As hard up for conversation as an invalid without his operation. Give him peace and you'd bury your husband. What can he listen to in this great frozen institution except the sound of his own eternal irritation? (*He claps him on the shoulder.*) Keep going, Headmaster, go off every minute. You're the dear old fog horn that lets us know we're still afloat.

LILY. Ssh. Caroline!

> ARTHUR *has raised his two clenched fists and now opens his hands and pushes himself up from the table.*

ARTHUR. She's been out for a walk.

> CAROLINE *has come in through the French window halfway through* TONY'S *speech. Now she closes them and comes into the room, crosses it, and hangs her mackintosh on the back of the door that leads to the school.*

(*Pulling out his watch and looking at it.*) She usually does at this time.

> CAROLINE *comes up to the three of them, and looks at them without expression. She sits down. The others stand. She is eighteen and extremely beautiful, her beauty being such that*

it is strange, composed and vaguely alarming. She has a look of complete innocence and wears, unexpectedly the sort of clothes worn by starlets on the covers of very cheap film magazines. These clothes have an appearance of being home made. She does not speak. While she is on the stage the other characters speak faster as if to conceal the fact of her silence from themselves.

TONY. I wonder where she's been?

LILY. Usually along the front.

TONY. She doesn't feel the cold?

ARTHUR. Brought up here, of course she doesn't notice it.

TONY. She always walks alone?

LILY. Hardly ever picks up a friend.

Pause while they all think of something to say. CAROLINE *is still expressionless.*

ARTHUR. Well – she's back just in time.

TONY. Haven't you got something to say to her?

ARTHUR. You needn't remind me. Many happy returns of the day.

He puts his hand out. CAROLINE *shakes it. Arthur sits down at the table.*

TONY. Many, many, happies, Caroline dear. (*He stoops to kiss the top of her head.*)

CAROLINE *lifts her face and kisses him on the mouth. She is still expressionless. He sits down, disconcerted, patting his lips with his handkerchief.*

LILY. Caroline, my baby. Don't grow up any more.

LILY *hugs* CAROLINE *like a child and then sits down.*

ARTHUR. She didn't like you saying that.

TONY. She didn't mind.

Pause while LILY *begins to cry.*

ARTHUR (*suddenly loses his temper*). Will you provoke me, Bin, with these bloody waterworks?

TONY. Look. She hasn't noticed her presents yet.

ARTHUR. She was upset.

TONY. No she wasn't.

CAROLINE *looks down at her place and lifts her hands in amazement. Her face is still without expression.*

LILY (*recovering*). She's seen them now.

ARTHUR (*eagerly*). She may open mine first.

TONY. Well, of all the selfish . . .

ARTHUR. She's going to. I hope you didn't notice me buying it, Caroline, in the High Street yesterday. Creeping out of W. H. Smith's.

TONY. Now you've given the game away.

ARTHUR. What are you hinting?

TONY. The mention of W. H. Smith. Now she can rule out stockings or underwear or any nice toilet water.

CAROLINE *shakes the parcel.*

TONY. Now she's guessed what it is.

ARTHUR. I don't believe she has.

CAROLINE *shakes her head.*

ARTHUR. No, she hasn't.

CAROLINE *opens the parcel, it contains a Halma set and three boy's adventure books.*

TONY. Same old things. She's bored with Halma.

ARTHUR. No she's not!

TONY. Yes she is.

ARTHUR. Anyway it's a wholesome game, Peters, unlike the indoor sports you're addicted to.

TONY. And these books! You only buy them to read them yourself. Three midshipmen stranded on a desert island. (*Picks up one and starts to read.*) 'Give over tickling, Harry, giggled his chum, little guessing it was the hairy baboon that had crept up behind the unsuspecting youngsters. . . .'

ARTHUR. She appreciates it.

LILY (*soothingly*). Of course she does, don't let's quarrel. Not on the birthday.

TONY (*putting down the book*). I suppose it takes all tastes.

LILY. Perhaps now she'll open mine.

CAROLINE *picks up a parcel.*

LILY. I made it for you, dear. It took so long. I seem to have been making it all my life.

CAROLINE *opens the parcel. A long sweater, white and endless with the school colours at the neck. She holds it in front of herself. It's far too long.*

LILY. Oh Caroline. There's too much of it. I had far too much spare time.

TONY (*putting his hand on* LILY's *shoulder*). She likes it. She thinks it'll keep her warm.

ARTHUR. Warm? Keep her warm did you say? I tell you its perfectly warm here, all the year round.

TONY. There now, Headmaster. Lily's right. We shouldn't quarrel on the birthday. And look. She's knitted in the school colours. That'll cheer you up, you know. When you see those colours always round your daughter.

ARTHUR. At least it shows some sense of loyalty.

TONY. Of course, not being, strictly speaking, a parent my present, gets opened last.

ARTHUR (*resentfully*). A treat saved up for you.

CAROLINE *picks up* TONY's *present. Holds it against her cheek. Listens to it.*

TONY. I believe. . . . Yes. I think I am right in saying (*radio commentator's voice*). 'The ceremony is just about to begin. It's a wonderful spectacle here to-day. The lady Mayoress has released the pigeons. The massed bands are striking up. The Boy Scouts are fainting in unprecedented numbers and . . .'

> CAROLINE *undoes the parcel, produces a gilt powder compact.*

ARTHUR. What can it be?

> CAROLINE *opens the compact and sprinkles powder on her nose.*

LILY. My baby. . . .

ARTHUR. Take that muck off your face. I forbid it. Go straight upstairs and wash.

TONY. Headmaster!

LILY. Surely Tony. She's still too young.

> TONY *goes behind* CAROLINE, *his hands on each side of her head he directs her face to one parent, then another.*

TONY. Can you be such unobservant parents? Your daughter has now been using cosmetics in considerable quantities for many years.

ARTHUR. Is this true, Bin?

LILY. She's still a child.

TONY. Her table upstairs is covered with tubes, little brushes and the feet of rabbits. In an afternoon, with nothing better to do, she can turn from a pale, coal eyed, fourteenth wife of an oil sheik to a brash, healthy, dog-keeping, pony-riding, daddy-adoring virgin with a pillar box mouth. Her beauty spots come off on the face towels and when she cries she cries black tears.

ARTHUR. Your appalling influence.

TONY. The passage of time, Headmaster. What can you and I do to prevent it?

ARTHUR. I see her as a little girl.

TONY. Then you don't bother to look.

ARTHUR. Did *you* notice Bin?

LILY. When the sun falls straight on her I do have my suspicions. We've had so little sun lately.

> *The clock groans and strikes.* CAROLINE *puts down the powder compact and goes out of the room, through the door to the boy's department.*

She's gone.

TONY. To collect her presents from the boys.

ARTHUR. Of course. I was forgetting.

TONY. She always does that next. Then she comes back to show us what they've given.

ARTHUR. Of course . . . of course.

> ARTHUR *and* LILY *are staring thoughtfully in front of them.* TONY *walks about nervously, about to broach a difficult subject.*

TONY. My old friends. (*He gets no reaction and starts again.*) Colleagues. Of course I'm not a parent.

ARTHUR (*angrily*). If only I could be sure of that.

TONY (*smiling flattered*). Not in any official sense. But I have at least been a child.

LILY (*looking at him affectionately*). Yes, Tony, of course you have.

TONY. Now frankly speaking, isn't eighteen a bit of a cross roads? Isn't there something, can't you feel, that Caroline ought to be told?

ARTHUR. Told?

TONY. Yes.

LILY. What sort of thing, Tony, had you in mind?

TONY (*suddenly at a loss*). We must have *something* to tell her.

At least I should have thought so. Nothing to embarass any one to tell, of course. . . . But (*more positive*) . . . her *education*. Aren't there a few gaps there?

ARTHUR. You don't find everything in the covers of books, Peters. That's why I always lay the emphasis on organized games.

TONY. Yes. I noticed. (*He picks up his ukelele and begins to play odd notes, tuning it as he speaks, more vaguely and with less assurance.*)

> LILY *goes out and, during* TONY'S *speech, comes back with a tray, including a dish of sausages and mash which she puts down to keep warm by the electric fire.*

It's not that I'm all that keen on education myself. In fact I merely drifted into it. It was a thé dansant on the river, Maidenhead. The waiter was feeding the swans, he had an apron full of bread crumbs. I was dancing with a girl called Fay Knockbroker. She was so small and yellow and it was hot to touch her. Like a red hot buttercup.

> ARTHUR *makes an explosion of disgust.* LILY *looks up at him from the dishes and smiles and goes out again.*

. . . 'Tony', she said, 'Why don't you do something? Why don't you work?' It appeared her father Knockbroker, what did he deal in, taps? – I really forget, has said marriage was forbidden unless I worked. I had five shillings in my trousers that afternoon. I couldn't have covered the cucumber sandwiches.

ARTHUR. Grossly irresponsible.

TONY. In fact marriage, was far from my thoughts. I only wanted to get Fay launched in a punt and pushed out under the willows.

ARTHUR. Disgusting.

TONY. Probably. But it's that punt, those willows, that have kept me going in all our cold winters.

LILY *comes in again with the tomato ketchup.*

That and. . . .

ARTHUR. Don't say it! I can guess. . . .

TONY. How do you live, Headmaster, without any of those old past moments to warm you up?

ARTHUR. I have my memories. A cry from the megaphone on the tow path. A cheer under Barnes Bridge.

TONY. But Miss Knockbroker wasn't stepping on board that afternoon. 'You get a job,' she said, 'or I stay on dry land and marry Humphrey Ewart. He works!'

ARTHUR (*interested grudgingly*). Did he?

TONY. She met him at the Guards' Boat Club. Blowing safes turned out to be his profession. Knockbroker was very livid when it all came out after the marriage.

ARTHUR. And you?

TONY. I went up to London to get a job. I had to leave her to pay for tea. What could I do? I didn't know anything. I had to teach. I had no great enthusiasm for education. I might have come to love it. As tutor cramming a young millionaire in the South of France, with his widowed mother bringing us long pink drinks to wash down the logarithms. . . .

ARTHUR (*suddenly roaring with laughter*). And you ended out here!

TONY. I only came temporarily. Till something else offered.

ARTHUR. You are still temporary. As far as I'm concerned.

LILY. You don't regret it Tony?

TONY (*looking round at her, then brassly*). Of course not. No regrets. I've no enthusiasm for education. But I can't help thinking. There are things Caroline should be *told*.

ARTHUR. What for instance?

TONY. We've had experience of life.

LILY (*lovingly*). Ah yes. How very true. Great experience of life.

TONY. Now, shouldn't we be passing on that experience to her?

ARTHUR. I'm against passing on experience. Boys find it very embarrassing.

TONY. But Caroline, Headmaster, isn't this rather the point we have to face? Is not, and can never be, barring all accidents, a boy.

ARTHUR. The principle's the same. I have it so often in class. You start by telling them something unimportant like the date of the Spanish Armada, 1585.

TONY. 1582.

ARTHUR. 1585.

TONY. 1582.

ARTHUR. Fifteen hundred and eighty five. The year of our Lord.

LILY. What can it matter after all these years?

ARTHUR. Imbecile. Don't interrupt me. Of course it matters. It's the mental discipline.

TONY. All right, Headmaster. Have it your own way. 1585.

ARTHUR. 1585. You start to tell them. . . . The Battle of the Armada. When England's Virgin Queen. . . . Then you've laid yourself open. . . .

TONY (*imitating*). Sir! What's a virgin?

ARTHUR. You see! It's most undesirable. The lesson may have half an hour to go, and if you start telling them about virgins where will you be when it's time to ring the bell? Know what I do Peters, if any questions of that type come up?

TONY. Yes. I do.

ARTHUR. I run straight out of the room and ring the bell myself. And that's my advice to you.

LILY. I suppose it's natural for them, to be curious.

TONY. They don't ask any questions unless they already know the answers.

ARTHUR *gets up and walks about, gradually working himself into a rage again.*

ARTHUR. That's purely cynical. Their minds are delightfully blank. That's how it's got to stay, it's the only way for Caroline. You start it, Peters. You feed her with bits of geography and history and mathematics. What comes next? Little scraps of information from you about Maidenhead and the Earls Court Road. Little tips from Bin on how to make love to another man while your husband's upstairs dressing. Little hints from both of you about face powder and silk stockings, free love and Queen Elizabeth and birth control and decimals and vulgar fractions and punts under the willow tree and she'll be down the slope – woosh! on the toboggan and you'll never stop her until she crashes into the great black iron railings of the answer which, please God, she mustn't ever know.

TONY. Which one is that?

ARTHUR. That ever since you came here and met Caroline's mother this decent school has been turned into a brothel! A corrupt . . .

He stops at the sound of a baby crying off stage.

What ever?

The baby cries again.

LILY (*delighted*). A baby crying.

TONY. One of the boys has asked the right question at last.

CAROLINE *wanders in from the boys' door, her arms full of jokes. She stops by* ARTHUR *and hands him the cardboard box which, when she turns it upside down, cries like a baby.* ARTHUR *turns it and it yells. He slowly relaxes.*

LILY. It's just a joke. . . .

TONY. One of her presents from the boys.

ARTHUR. How very, very amusing.

TONY. How strange these boys are.

CAROLINE *hands* TONY *a bottle of beer. He tries to open it and finds its made of rubber.* LILY *gets a squeaking banana.* CAROLINE *has a pair of glasses which include a nose and teeth which she puts on. They all sit down,* CAROLINE *quite motionless in her false nose, the others urgently talking.*

TONY. Will you light the candles, Headmaster? Give a warm, shaded, Café Royal touch to the proceedings.

ARTHUR (*lighting the candles*). Sausages and mash I see.

LILY (*serving it out*). And red jelly to follow.

ARTHUR. Always Caroline's favourite men⁻

TONY. Since she was twelve.

ARTHUR. That's why we always put it on for the birthday.

LILY. It marks the occasion.

ARTHUR. When I was a boy my birthday always fell when I was away from home at Cadet camp. My old aunt gave me my cake to take in a tin. I had to keep it under my camp bed until the day came, then I'd get it out and eat it.

LILY. Let's be grateful. Caroline doesn't have to go to Cadet camp. She can birthday at home.

ARTHUR. As often as not when I came to open that tin the bird had flown.

TONY. Poor old Headmaster. I never knew that about you.

ARTHUR. Odd thing about it. I suspected that chaplain.

TONY. Not of scoffing your cake?

ARTHUR. It's a fact. I couldn't get it out of my head. An effiminate sort of fellow, the chaplain. Welsh. And he had a sweet tooth.

LILY. I'm giving Caroline some more because it's her favourite dinner.

TONY. Yes. I see.

ARTHUR. It was terribly upsetting for a young boy in my position.

TONY. Indeed yes.

ARTHUR. You can't put your heart into Church Parade when

you suspect the padre of nibbling at your one and only birthday present.

TONY. Let's hope you misjudged him.

ARTHUR. I was a sound judge of character. He was a man who let the side down badly.

TONY. Suspicious of everyone. Even them.

ARTHUR. What are you trying to infer?

TONY. Nothing at all. Shall I do the honours again, Headmaster?

ARTHUR. Yes. And when you come to Caroline's glass.

TONY. What?

ARTHUR. Fill it up.

LILY. With alcohol? She won't like it.

TONY *fills* CAROLINE'S *glass. She drains it thirstily.*

TONY. There, Lily. It appears you were wrong.

ARTHUR. Thinking it over, Peters, I have thought your earlier remarks weren't entirely senseless. Caroline *has* reached a turning point. The time has come when she can be invited to join her father and mother in a light stimulant. It's a privilege, and like all privileges it brings new responsibilities.

TONY. In my humble opinion there are very few responsibilities involved in a glass of beer.

ARTHUR. There are responsibilities in everything, running a school, getting married, living at all. That's what we've got to tell Caroline. She's got to have faith in something bigger than herself.

LILY. Caroline's a woman now. Isn't that right, Tony? Didn't you say that?

TONY. Almost a woman, I should say.

LILY. Then there are things only a woman can tell her?

ARTHUR. There are bigger things in life than knitting patterns and . . . bottling fruit.

I means there *are* things a person can sacrifice himself for.

The side. The school. The right comrades, sweating at the
oar.

TONY. There speaks the cox of the West Woolwich rowing
club.

ARTHUR. Will you mock everything Peters?

TONY. The small man yelling through a paper megaphone
while the comrades lug themselves to death at forty from
fatty degeneration of the heart.

ARTHUR. Is nothing to be sacred?

TONY. There are better ways of getting heart failure.

ARTHUR. It all comes down to *that*.

TONY. Caroline's young. Every day she should collect some
small pleasure, to keep her warm when the years begin to
empty out. She should try everything, and not mind making
mistakes. When she reaches our age it won't be her mistakes
she'll regret. . . .

ARTHUR. What are you telling her?

TONY. When I remember those girls at Maidenhead, their
thumbs up, their faces smiling, doing the Lambeth Walk. . . .
It's not the ones I got away for the weekend I regret. It's
the ones I never had the courage to ask.

ARTHUR. I was trying to give Caroline something to believe in,
and you will everlastingly chip in with your unsavoury
reminiscences. . . .

TONY. Headmaster, are we attempting too much? Suppose we
just give her some accurate information. Such as . . . where
Gibraltar is.

ARTHUR. Gibraltar?

TONY. Yes. Go on. Tell her.

ARTHUR. At the bottom of Spain.

TONY. The bottom?

ARTHUR. Coming round the corner. Cadiz on the right.

TONY. You mean the right?

ARTHUR. The left then. Malaga on the right. Do I mean the
left?

TONY. Headmaster. Are you sure you have any information to transfer?

ARTHUR. All right Peters. (*Getting up.*) You've managed it. You've cast a blight. You've had your mockery. You've sneered at the most respected club on the river. You've spoiled the birthday for me now. I'm not staying. It's no use beseeching.

TONY. But Headmaster.

ARTHUR. You've rubbed the bloom off the birthday for me. I'm leaving you two together. Remember – a child is watching.

He goes out slamming the door to the bedrooms.

LILY. He's gone.

TONY. Yes.

CAROLINE *sighs and sits down in the basket chair.*

TONY. If only he wouldn't take it as such a personal matter. It's not my fault where they put Gibraltar. (*He picks up the ukelele and tunes it.*)

LILY. Ssh. Caroline's expecting a song.

TONY. An old one. . . .

LILY. That Turk and the extraordinary Russian?

TONY (*singing*).

'Oh the sons of the prophet are hardy and bold
And quite unaccustomed to fear,
But the greatest by far
In the courts of the Shah –
Was Abdul the Bul Bul Emir.'

LILY. Of course Caroline adores this one. . . .

TONY. 'If they wanted a man to encourage the van or shout. . . .'

LILY (*shouts*). 'Atta boy.'

TONY.   'In the rear
Without any doubt
They always sent out. . . .'

Damn. I almost forgot. I owe the pub for those whiffs. I'm duty bound to slip back.

LILY. Oh Tony.

TONY. They were an expensive gesture. . . .

LILY. Have a look in that box. The egg money. . . .

TONY *finds five shillings in a box on the mantelpiece. Pockets it in triumph.*

LILY. Must you go tonight?

TONY (*dramatic voice stifling sobs, tough American accent*). 'I'm only a small guy, not very brave. I guess this is just one of the things that comes to a small guy and well, he's just got to go through with it if he ever wants to be able to shake his own hand again this side of the Great River. Maybe if I go through with this Lily, hundreds of little guys all over the world are going to be safe to shake their own hands and look themselves in the whites of their eyes. Maybe if I don't they won't. Kinda hard to tell. (*Looks out of the French window.*) It's just about sun up time. Guess Arthur Loudon's boys are sawing off their shot guns 'bout now down there in the alfafa. So long folks. If ma sobers up tell her Goodbye. Let's hit the trail now. Don't forget the empties. (*He hitches up his trousers, picks up the string bag of empties and lurches out of the French window.*)

LILY *is laughing hard.* CAROLINE *is quite impassive.*

TONY (*off stage*). Bang, bang, bang.

LILY. Tony, you'll kill me.

TONY (*staggering in backwards, his hand on his heart*). They killed me too, honey. Tell ma I'm feeling just fine, can't hardly notice the difference. (*Looks religiously upwards.*) O.K. Mr Gabriel Archangel. I heard you. I'm a coming. Maybe take a little time on account of this old webbed foot of mine.'

Limps out of French window.

F

LILY. Oh Tony Peters. What should I do without you?

Pause.

Caroline, they try to tell you things – but what can they tell you? We're not men you see, we're something different. Lots of men don't realize that. All men except, except Tony.

CAROLINE *still sits impassively.* LILY *kneels on the floor in front of her.*

LILY. I'm a woman, Caroline. And you're going to be one as well. Nothing can stop you. I'm a woman and what does Arthur call me? He calls me Bin. Bin, when my name is Lily. Now does Bin sound like a woman's name to you? You know why he calls me Bin? Because he wants me to be his friend, his assistant, his colleague, his thoroughly good chap. To rough it with him on a walking tour through life. He's said that to me, Caroline. How can I be a good chap, I wasn't born a chap. *My sex gets in the way.* That's why he gets so angry. (*She gets up and moves about the room.*) Look Caroline, do you know why he calls me Bin? Because my father did and my uncle did and so did my five brothers who all married soft hearted tittering girls in fluffy pullovers which came off on them like falling hair and white peep toe shoes and had pet names for their hot water bottles. Those brothers called me Bin. Good old Bin, you can put her on the back of the motor bike. Bin's marvellous, she can go in the dicky because her hair's always in a tangle and her cheeks are like bricks and the wind can't do her any harm, but Babs or Topsy or Melanie has to sit in front because she's such a fuss pot and so I can change gear next to her baby pink and artificial silk and get her angora all tied up in my Harris tweed. If you take Bin out it's for great slopping pints and the other one about the honeymoon couple in the French hotel, and then you can be sick in the hedge on the way because Bin's a good chap. We're women Caroline. They buy us beer when we long to order protection and flattery and excitement and crème de menthe and little bottles of sparkling wine with silver paper tops and oh God, we long to be kept warm. Aren't I right? Isn't that how we feel? Mothers and daughters and wives. . . . (*Kneeling again.*) Oh Caroline tell me I'm right. Caroline. Speak to us. What have we done wrong?

> CAROLINE *says nothing, but, for the first time she smiles slowly and puts her hands on her mother's shoulder.* LILY *gets up, gets the tray which she has left leaning against the wall and begins to stack the plates.*

LILY. Anyway all my friends got married and there was only Arthur. He was small and violent and believed in everything. Life wasn't much fun at home, my brothers got married and their wives refused to take on their pets. After the youngest left I was walking out with five Alsatian dogs. Father economized on the wedding. 'We needn't hire a car for Bin,' he said. My brother Tommy took me to the church on the back of his motor bike. My first long dress and I was rushed up to my wedding wearing goggles and waving in the wind like a flag. We're women, Caroline. There's supposed to be a mystery about us. We should be sprung on our men like a small surprise in the warmth and darkness of the night – not delivered by a boy on a motor bike like a parcel that's come undone in the post. It shouldn't be like that for you Caroline. The day after the marriage I told Arthur I loved him. 'There are more important things than love,' he said. 'What more important things?' 'Companionship,' he said, 'helping one another. Now we're dedicated, our lives are dedicated.' 'What to?' I asked him. 'The boys.' Can you believe it? Those dreadful children coughing like old sheep upstairs. I was dedicated to *them*. I went to look at them. They were in striped pyjamas, they looked like little old convicts with cropped heads and match-stick arms and legs.

They had hard, sexless voices and the faint, cold smell of lead pencils. And you know what? Arthur said it would make them think of me as more of a sport. He told them to call me Bin. I ask you. Is that a name for a woman?

ARTHUR (*shouts off stage*). What are you doing, Bin?

LILY (*suddenly shouts back*). *Clearing away.* (*Then quietly.*) That day was so empty. It seemed I'd been born a woman for nothing at all. Yet I couldn't be a man. Arthur wanted me to play cricket with the boys – can you imagine that Caroline? My legs were still young, and his idea was to see them buckled up in cricketing pads. My soft hands in the gloves of a wicket keeper. . . .

ARTHUR (*off stage shouts*). I heard singing. Then the singing stopped. What's he got round to now?

LILY. I was a woman and there was no time for me.

ARTHUR (*off stage*). Don't you realize? I went to bed because of the way you all treated me. I can't get out again. It'd be ridiculous!

LILY (*shouts*). I'll be up in a minute. (*Quiet.*) Just a succession of days. Saints' Days with no lessons before breakfast. Sundays when the boys hit each other in the evening. Mondays when Arthur loses his temper. Nothing. Like a party when no one's remembered to send out the invitation. . . . Then Tony came. . . .

She leaves the dishes stacked on the tray and sits near CAROLINE.

ARTHUR. Bin! Come here, Bin! Don't leave me alone.

LILY. You know Tony can never be serious. Perhaps he's not very honest. Does he speak the truth all the time? I don't care. He treats me as if I was born to be a woman. Lily, Lily, all the time and never a nickname. And he's made Arthur jealous. (*Triumphant.*) *They quarrel over me Caroline. They've been fighting over me for years.* Imagine that! Good old Bin. She won't mind going home alone now we've met you girls. . . .

LILY *gets up. Turns to the middle of the room.*

But now it's Lily Loudon and Arthur's developed jealousy.

ARTHUR (*shouting off stage*). Are you going to rob me of my sleep? It's the semi-finals tomorrow.

LILY (*shouting*). What semi-finals?

ARTHUR (*shouting back*). Squash. Masters v Boys.

LILY (*contemptuously*). Squash! What did Tony say today? 'Lily,' always Lily you see, 'needs no half light to look perpetually beautiful.' He said that. A man with all those available telephone numbers.

ARTHUR (*plaintifully off*). The boys'll make a fool of me if I don't get some sleep.

LILY. It'll come to you Caroline. If you're a woman it's bound to come. In the middle of the afternoon, perhaps. During cricket practice. You'll hear a sound in the gravel, someone singing outside the window. You stand quite still holding your breath in case they should go away. And then, when the windows opens. . . . Caroline, I'm telling you. It's the only thing that matters. . . .

ARTHUR (*shouts*). Am I never to see you again?

LILY. One day he'll do his insides mischief, shouting like that Just put the tray in the kitchen would you. We'll wash up in the morning. I shouldn't have told you all that. I've enjoyed it though, telling myself. Don't remember it all. Only remember you're Caroline – make them call you that. Don't let them call you a funny name.

ARTHUR (*off stage*). Bin!

LILY. Coming Arthur. I'm coming now.

> *She looks at* CAROLINE *and then goes out of the door.* CAR-
> OLINE *sighs, stretches and then gets up and carries the tray
> out of the room. The stage is empty.* CAROLINE *comes back
> and looks round the room. She takes out her powder compact.
> Standing over by the mantelpiece, powders her nose She
> puts out the light. The stage is dark, only the electric fire*

glowing. She draws the curtains in front of the French window showing a square of grey moonlight. She goes and sits down to wait. She waits. There's a footstep. She stands, her arms outstretched.

TONY (*off stage, singing*).

'. . . . "Do you hold life so dull.
That you're seeking to end your career?"
Vile infidel know
You have trod on the toe . . .'

TONY *comes in at the French window. Stumbles in the darkness.*

What's up? Everyone gone to bed?

CAROLINE *makes a slight sound and falls on him, her arms round his neck, her mouth pressed on his. In the square of moonlit French window he is struggling to release his neck from her hands. When he frees himself he dashes to the door and switches on the light.*

TONY. Caroline. What have they been telling you now?

She moves towards him.

Whatever it was – you can't have understood. You must have got it wrong.

He opens the door behind him. He disappears rapidly through the door. CAROLINE *faces the audience. She is not unduly upset. Her hands turn palm outwards, she heaves a small sigh, her eyes turn upwards in mock despair. On her, the Curtain slowly falls.*

Scene Two

Early evening, the next day. The table is laid with an assortment of tea cups and plates. CAROLINE *is alone, reading a letter propped up on the tea pot in front of her. She looks very pleased, as she folds up the letter and puts it in a pocket of her skirt.*

She gets up and goes over to the roll top desk. In wrestling to get a suitcase from behind it she knocks over the globe.

ARTHUR (*shouting off stage, from the right*). What's that for mercy's sake?

> CAROLINE *brings out the battered suitcase and takes it over to the hearth rug where she opens it and begins to drop in the presents which she has arranged on the mantelpiece.*

(*Shouts.*) Bin. Is that you?

> CAROLINE *drops in the baby crier which screams in the case.*

What are you playing at you imbecile?

> CAROLINE *shuts the case.* TONY *appears outside the French windows and starts to haul down the flag.* CAROLINE *crosses the room, and, as he comes in, hastily puts her suitcase outside the door that leads to the boys' department.*

ARTHUR (*off*). Who is it, burglars? Answer me, Bin.
TONY (*folding up the Union Jack*). It may be a silly business but it pleases the headmaster. Caroline. I wanted to talk. Couldn't we talk. I promise you ... I haven't slept. I believe, I feel sure ... we could ... both ... talk.

> CAROLINE *exits through the boys' door.* ARTHUR *bursts into the room putting on his coat.*

ARTHUR. I heard you Peters. Make no mistake about that. . . .

> TONY *folds up the Union Jack, puts it on the desk and goes over to the table, sits down and pours himself out a cup of tea. He looks very tired.*

TONY. I've never felt it before, Headmaster. It never really took hold of me till now.

ARTHUR. Not to speak can be just as deceptive as lying, Peters. There's an awful, deceptive silence about people in this house, a goading, tormenting, blank silence. Every question I shout is like sending a soldier into the dark night of a silent, enemy country.

TONY. Have a cup of tea?

ARTHUR. Were you in here with her?

TONY. They sat in front of me, rows of boys. Usually I feel quite indifferent about them, as if they were rows of strangers sitting opposite me in a train. I merely want to avoid conversation with them until the bell rings and we can all get out at the station.

ARTHUR. What were you two doing, banging about in here? Shall I never know the truth?

TONY. Sit down and have some tea. All that shouting must leave you parched.

ARTHUR. How can I spare my voice? Leading this sort of life, I mean.

> *He sits down.* TONY *pours him tea.*

TONY. It's hard for you, I do appreciate.

ARTHUR. But you're the one reason for my shouting. . . .

TONY. Let me try and explain. There they sat, these children, with the pale look of old age hanging around them – of course they're much older than us, Headmaster, you do realize that don't you?

ARTHUR. Older?

TONY. And before they are finally taken away, done up in

blankets, muffled in scarves, tweed caps balanced on their ancient heads, to institutions, I felt there was something I ought to tell them. Only . . .

ARTHUR. Yes?

TONY. I couldn't for the life of me remember what it was. But if you don't tell children anything. . . .

ARTHUR. Well?

TONY. They get some extraordinary ideas.

ARTHUR. What do you mean?

TONY. I'm not sure if I'm in a position to tell you. All I can say is that I've had a shock, a pretty severe shock as it so happens, in the last twenty-four hours. I tell you, I don't often get a jolt like that these days. Last night, I say this quite frankly, sleep eluded me.

ARTHUR. Well, of course.

TONY. What do you mean, 'Well of course'?

ARTHUR. Missing Bin, weren't you?

TONY. Not at the time.

ARTHUR. I winkled her away from you.

TONY. Did you now?

ARTHUR. Brought her up to bed when you least expected it.

TONY. Oh, I see.

ARTHUR. My God, I'd liked to have seen the bewildered expression on your face when you found your beautiful bird – caged for the night.

TONY. Look, Headmaster, this shock I was referring to, it's made me think – well, I feel we shall have to face things as they are at very long last. Now I know this business has been a source of considerable interest and excitement to us all over a long period of years. It's kept us going, as you might say, when the results of the squash rackets competition and the state of the weather and the suspicion about who pinched the nail brush off the chain in the downstairs loo have been powerless to quicken the pulse. But it's gone too far, you know – we should never have started it.

ARTHUR. Of course you shouldn't. Now there's a twinge of conscience.

TONY. You know as much as I do. There's never been a breath of anything amiss.

ARTHUR (*singing bitterly*). 'Tell me the old, old, story. . . .'

TONY. It started as an occupation. Like Halma or sardines. It's kept us from growing old.

ARTHUR. Bluff your way out of it, like when the waiter comes with the bill and 'Most unfortunately my cheque book caught fire in my overcoat pocket'.

TONY. Must we go on pretending? I don't even fancy Lily. Hardly my type.

ARTHUR (*aghast*). What are you saying?

TONY. That I don't love your wife. . . .

ARTHUR. You don't?

TONY. And never have.

ARTHUR (*with quiet fury*). You unspeakable hound! (*Beginning to shout.*) You don't love her? My God, I ought to strike you Peters.

TONY. That young Fay Knockbroker remains my ideal. Small and yellow and red hot. The girl you have to keep on protecting from the wicked results of her own innocence.

ARTHUR. But Bin. . . .

TONY. Not my sort at all. A very decent, understanding sort, naturally: but the sort you'd always cram into the dicky if you had a girl like Fay to ride with in front.

ARTHUR. You don't love Bin?

TONY. I'm afraid not. . . .

ARTHUR. She's given you the best years of her life. . . .

TONY. Really, Headmaster . . . I feel we ought to face these facts squarely . . . otherwise . . . well it may have, perhaps it's already had . . . results we didn't foresee.

ARTHUR. Bin. Poor girl. She mustn't ever guess.

TONY (*gently*). You are . . . fond of your wife, Headmaster?

ARTHUR. Fond of her. I *love* her, Peters. When I married I

expected it would be for companionship – I'd known friendship before, Peters, genuine friendship. Someone to tramp around Wales with, to give a fill from your pouch, to share a hunk of cold Christmas pudding on a Boxing Day morning by Beachy Head – marriage is different, Peters. It takes place with a *woman*.

TONY. So I've been led to believe.

ARTHUR. And with a woman as attractive, soft, yielding, feminine as my Bin.

TONY. You take that view of her?

ARTHUR. Who mustn't ever be hurt ... Oh it's hard. I tell you that at once, Peters, to live with such a feminine person as a woman in your life.

TONY. Problems arise of course.

ARTHUR. We had our work to do. We had the school to serve. Our lives aren't ours I told her. We're dedicated to the boys. And all the time all I wanted was to stay in bed with her all day only occasionally getting up for bread and marmalade.

TONY. Really. (*A long, embarrassed pause.*)

ARTHUR. Women are sensitive creatures, Peters. Lily mustn't be allowed to guess at what you've just told me.

TONY (*gestures resignedly*). But it's led to this. . . .

ARTHUR. She mustn't be *hurt*. Lily must never be *hurt*.

Pause.

TONY. You'll perhaps resent my saying this Arthur, and that's the risk I'm bound to take. But if you don't want Lily hurt ... sometimes I'm bound to notice. . . .

ARTHUR (*proudly*). I shout at her you mean?

TONY. Well, not exactly coo.

ARTHUR. That's love. . . .

TONY. Oh yes?

ARTHUR. It takes people in different ways. Now when *you* want to make love to her I've noticed. . . .

TONY. But really!

ARTHUR. You make a joke. You pretend to be at the North Pole. You sing a song.

TONY. My weakness: I'm not serious.

ARTHUR. But when I see all that I love about my wife. The way she twists the hair over her ears when the time comes to make out a list. The soft smile she gives when no one's looking. How she shuts in laughter with the palm of her hand. . . . Then, I feel so small and angry. I see myself so powerless, so drawn into her that once I let myself go, all I believe in, all I'm dedicated to would be spent on afternoons of bread and marmalade. Then I shout. I don't know why it is. The terms of endearment I'm meaning to say just come out screaming. Is it a natural reaction?

TONY. I hardly know.

ARTHUR. And the agony of being in a room without her. The doubt and the anxiety that she'll be taken from me by the time I get back.

TONY. Really. We've got to stop it. This performance of ours has had its influence on Caroline. . . .

ARTHUR. Caroline? She's innocent of it all. She doesn't enter . . .

TONY. It has to stop, Headmaster.

ARTHUR. Who's going to stop it?

TONY. I am.

ARTHUR. You couldn't stop a catch.

TONY. I'm in duty bound. . . . (*Standing up.*)

ARTHUR. To tell Bin you don't love her. . . .

TONY. To tell the truth. For Caroline.

ARTHUR (*standing up, facing him*). Tony Peters. I need you. I know I have a sense of dedication which my wife doesn't altogether understand. In a way I'm a hard row for a woman like Bin to furrow. I shout. I'm a prey to irritation. I can't imitate snowstorms. I've forgotten all the jokes I've ever heard. She needs the bright lights, Peters, the music. The interest of another man. I knew that soon after I married her.

I can't tell you how relieved I was the day you walked
through those French windows. Then I knew my married
life was safe at last.

TONY (*sitting down, bewildered*). Headmaster. This is a thought
I would have put well beyond you.

ARTHUR (*solicitous*). I've shocked you?

TONY. Deeply. Deeply shocked.

ARTHUR. Together, all these years, we've kept Lily so happy.

TONY. You seem, Headmaster, to have the most tenuous grasp
of morality.

ARTHUR. My temper and your songs – what a crowded, event-
ful time we've given her. And you must confess, Peters, it's
been an interest for you. I mean there can't still be so many
irons in your fire these days, whatever your part in Earls
Court may have been.

TONY. Oh, Headmaster. I don't know what you're trying to
find, but you're getting dangerously warm.

ARTHUR. We depend on each other, Peters. You mustn't tell
her. We all depend on each other. . . .

TONY. But the younger generation? What are we doing
for it?

ARTHUR. Our best, Peters. Let's allow ourselves that. . . .

TONY. But when I walked through these French windows. . . .

ARTHUR. You took on a job, Peters. You can't get out of it now.

TONY. I shouldn't have been singing. That was when I made
my great mistake. . . .

The kitchen door opens. LILY *enters smoking a cigarette,
carrying a plate of bread and butter.*

LILY. Has Caroline had her tea? I've been cutting all this bread
and butter. The trouble with living here, the butter gets as
hard as the rock of Gibraltar. It blasts great holes in your
sliced bread.

TONY. Don't mention Gibraltar, Lily.

ARTHUR. There you go. Trying to pretend it's cold.

LILY *drops cigarette ash on the bread, blows it off and sits down.*

LILY. Out in the kitchen I heard men's voices rising and falling, rising and falling. What've you two been talking about now?

TONY. About you.

LILY. How nice.

ARTHUR. Tony's confessed.

LILY. Confessed?

ARTHUR. What he feels about you.

LILY. What he feels. (*She looks delightedly at Tony*). Have you Tony? (*She's biting bread and butter and smoking at the same time.*) What did you say?

ARTHUR. Do you want to tell my wife, Peters? Do you want to put a stop to this whole business, once and for all?

They both look at him. TONY *gasps, smiles, and then gets up and walks up and down talking in clipped naval accents.*

TONY. 'Ladies and gentlemen. It is my duty to inform you that we have struck an iceberg. At nine-o-hundred hours, fish were noticed swimming in the first-class bath water. All ports have been alerted and in approximately ten-o-o hours they will start looking for us by helicopter. If the ship has already sunk we will rendezvous at latitude 9.700 and bob about in the water together as long as possible. . . .'

He comes to rest behind LILY'S *chair.*

Oh Lily. I can't tell you how complicated it's all become.

ARTHUR. No. You can't.

CAROLINE *enters from the boys' side, left. She is carrying her suitcase which she puts down on the floor.*

LILY. Caroline!

CAROLINE *unhooks her mackintosh from the back of the door*

and slowly puts it on. ARTHUR *and* LILY *watch her
fearfully. She picks up the suitcase and stands in front of the
French windows.*

ARTHUR. She's going for a walk.

LILY. Probably that's it.

TONY. Haven't you noticed the suitcase? Does she usually go
for a walk with a suitcase?

LILY. Caroline. Put it down.

She gets up and goes towards CAROLINE. TONY *puts out his
arm and stops her.*

TONY. Better to let her do what she wants.

LILY. What does she want? How can she tell us?

CAROLINE *opens her mouth. Long silence in which she is
making an enormous effort until she says –*

CAROLINE. I want to go to London.

They look at her in amazement. In dead silence CAROLINE
puts down her suitcase.

I've got a job with the Threadneedle Street Branch of the
Chesterfield and National Bank. I start at a salary of seven
pounds ten shillings a week.

She takes the letter and hands it to LILY. LILY *crying looks
at it and hands it to* ARTHUR. ARTHUR *reads it and gives it
to* TONY.

TONY. There seems to be some truth in what she says.

LILY. Stop her. Stop her leaving us, Arthur.

ARTHUR. She spoke. Our daughter spoke.

TONY *gives* CAROLINE *back the letter.*

CAROLINE. I have a third floor room at 109 Great Bidford
Street which costs four pounds ten shillings a week, with

board. I shall therefore have three pounds fifteen shillings a week left over. . . .

TONY. Caroline . . . I hate to disillusion you.

ARTHUR. She's talking. She's talking to me.

CAROLINE. Goodbye. (*She shakes* ARTHUR'S *hand.*)

ARTHUR. Forgive me.

CAROLINE. Goodbye. (*She shakes* LILY'S *hand.*)

LILY. What have we done wrong?

CAROLINE. Good-bye. (*She shakes* TONY'S *hand.*)

TONY. Good-bye.

LILY. It's too late to go now. . . .

CAROLINE. The train leaves at 7.15 from Coldsands Station. Platform One. Change at Norwich. (*She goes out and closes the French windows. For a moment she stands looking in at them through the glass. Then she disappears.*)

TONY. Let's hope she's right about that.

LILY. Why didn't you stop her?

ARTHUR (*sitting down*). She spoke to me. She said good-bye.

TONY. Well, that's right, she did.

LILY (*standing distractedly in the middle of the room*). What shall I do?

TONY. Clear away the tea.

ARTHUR. Lily. There's something you ought to know about Caroline. She hasn't said anything for a long time.

Silence. Then TONY *says.*

TONY. We'd noticed that.

ARTHUR. You didn't comment?

TONY *shrugs his shoulders.*

ARTHUR. You didn't like to?

TONY. It seemed unnecessary.

ARTHUR. Kindness held you back?

LILY. We must stop her going.

TONY. She won't meet any harm.

ARTHUR. But you don't know why she didn't speak? I told you, Peters, all the terms of endearment start shouting and screaming when I utter them. When I love someone all my love turns to irritation. I lost my temper with Caroline! I hit her! I actually hit her!

LILY (*crossing towards him*). No dear. You didn't.

ARTHUR. How do you know?

TONY. We were here in the room. You didn't hit her, Headmaster.

ARTHUR (*deflated*). I did. I wanted to hit her. After that, I thought she didn't speak. The nervous shock. Was it the nervous shock do you think, either of you?

LILY. Perhaps she didn't want to.

TONY. Or she had nothing to say to us. Although we had enough to say to her. . . .

LILY. Who shall we talk to now?

TONY. Each other, Lily. Always to each other.

LILY. Caroline! Why should she have to go, Tony?

TONY. She has to go sometime.

ARTHUR. I made her go. I hit her. I must have hit her. There's no other explanation.

TONY (*sits down in the basket-chair and picks up his ukelele*). How shall we ever know?

ARTHUR. What do you mean. For God's sake explain what you mean?

TONY. Was it your temper or her temper that stopped her speaking? Was it just the complete lack of interest that overcomes all children at the thought of the parents who gave them birth?

ARTHUR. I wasn't responsible?

TONY. What's responsible for Caroline as she is? What you told her? What you didn't tell her? The fact we told her a lie? The fact we told her the truth? Look back, Arthur. Look back, Lily do. What made us what we are? Anything our fathers and mothers said? More likely something that

G

happened when we were all alone. Something we thought of for ourselves, looking for a passable disguise in a dusty attic, or for a path that didn't exist in the hot summer in the middle of a wood that smelt of nettles.

ARTHUR. Is that how you found things out?

TONY. My dear old headmaster. I've never found out anything. I'm not a parent, but in my weak moments, like this afternoon, I've wanted to tell things to the young. Why do we do it? Not to give them information, but to make them repeat our lives. That's all. It's finished with us and we don't want it to be finished. We'd like them to do it for us – all over again. It'll be better for Caroline to work in the bank. If only her *adding* weren't quite so shaky. Let's hope she errs, Headmaster, on the side of generosity.

LILY *gets up and begins to put things on a tray.*

ARTHUR. What are you doing, Bin?

LILY. Clearing away the tea. (*She goes out with the tray.*)

TONY (*looking at his watch*). Just ten minutes and the boys have to stop their so called 'free time' and be hoarded into prep. I shall sit with them in silence. I'm not tempted to communicate with them any more.

ARTHUR. I'd better start to get the history corrected. Then I must take the roll-call. Let's hope the boys are all . . . still with us.

He goes over to the roll top desk. Starts marking exercise books.

TONY (*singing softly*).
          'Here we sit like birds in the wilderness,
             Birds in the wilderness.
             Birds in the wilderness.
          Here we sit like birds in the wilderness . . .'

ARTHUR. Peters.

TONY (*singing*). 'Down in Demerara. . . .'

ARTHUR. Was Henry the Third the *son* of Henry the Second?

TONY. He certainly wasn't his daughter.

ARTHUR. It doesn't *look* right somehow.

TONY. I suspect him of having been the son of King John.

ARTHUR. This boy misled me!

TONY. You can't rely on *them*. Not for accurate information.

ARTHUR. Peters.

TONY. Yes, Headmaster?

ARTHUR. Bin hasn't taken it too well, Caroline going off like that.

TONY. A loss for us all, of course.

ARTHUR. It's taken a great deal from her.

TONY. Yes.

ARTHUR. It's more important than ever. . . .

TONY. What is?

ARTHUR. That we should keep going. Like we always have. If we stopped quarrelling over her now. . . .

TONY. Yes Headmaster?

ARTHUR. Think how empty her poor life would be.

TONY. And our lives?

ARTHUR. Empty too, perhaps.

TONY. You know, it must be almost twenty years ago that I came in through that window and made a joke. And now, it seems, I've got to live on that joke for ever.

> LILY *comes in. She shivers, rubs her hands and crouches by the electric fire to warm them.*

LILY. It's cold.

ARTHUR. Nonsense.

LILY. It seems strange. Just the three of us. Shall we always be alone now?

ARTHUR. There it is.

TONY. You never know. Just when you felt most lonely in Earls Court I always noticed this, it was always the time when you met a bit of new. I remember feeling damned lonely one spring evening, about this time, walking down the

Earls Court Road, and there was this beautiful girl, about eighteen, no older than Caroline in fact, her gloved finger pressed to a bell.

ARTHUR. I hope there's nothing disgusting about this reminiscence Peters.

TONY. So I said nothing. I went and stood beside her. She gave me a glance. It wasn't exactly marching orders. Then the door was opened by another girl, slightly older. 'Come in darling,' she said. 'I'm so glad you could bring your husband.' So we sat us down to four courses and later as it came on to fog, it was carte blanche of the spare bedroom for the night. You see the hostess, it all turned out, had never seen the husband.

LILY. And that poor husband?

TONY. Unexpectedly lamed that very afternoon. A taxi had run over his foot, so she explained it in the spare room.

LILY. And you walked straight up to her?

TONY. Quick work wasn't it?

LILY. A quick worker, Tony.

TONY. No grass grows under Tony Peters, thank God.

ARTHUR. I made sure that story would end up as disgusting.

LILY. Oh Tony! What adventures you've had!

TONY. Adventures, thank goodness, still come to me.

He looks longingly at LILY. *She puts an elbow on his knee and gazes into the electric fire.*

ARTHUR. Isn't the room big enough? Do you have to sit on top of one another?

TONY. Now Headmaster. It'll soon be time for roll-call.

LILY (*thoughtfully*). I haven't really had many adventures. Have you, Arthur?

ARTHUR. What?

LILY. Had many adventures?

ARTHUR (*reading*). Was that Henry II?

TONY. Was what Henry II?

ARTHUR. The chap whose son was drowned?
TONY. Drowned?
ARTHUR. In the White Ship.

   TONY *picks up his ukelele and sings to* LILY.

TONY (*singing*).
            'Here we sit like birds in the wilderness,
            Birds in the wilderness.'
ARTHUR (*closing the exercise book and beginning to shout*). Peters.
   Bin. Stop goading me both of you. Don't you even wait now
   until I'm decently out of the room?
TONY (*singing*).
            'Here we sit like birds in the wilderness,
            Down in Demerara.
                  As the ship went down.'
ARTHUR (*standing up and hitting his desk with a tremendous
   crash with his fist*). Stop singing to my wife! Take your greedy
   eyes off her!

   ARTHUR *and* LILY *look at each other with deep affection.*
   TONY *plays a note on his ukelele.* ARTHUR *exits.*

                    Curtain

I Spy

First produced on the BBC Third Programme on 19th November, 1957, subsequently produced on BBC Television on 28th January, 1958.

The play was first performed on the stage at the Salisbury Playhouse on 16th March, 1959, with the following cast:

MR FRUTE	*Ronald Magill*
MRS MORGAN	*Nancie Herrod*
GLADYS	*Helen Dorward*
LAWYER	*Timothy West*
CAPTAIN MORGAN	*Tony Steedman*

Directed by Rolf Kruger

The action of the play passes on the promenade and in the serving- and dining-room of the Stag at Bay, in the seaside town of Cold Sands, Norfolk, and in a lawyer's office in London.

Time – the present.

The stage is divided into three acting areas. Back stage, against a clear background, a row of railings and a shelter represent the promenade of the seaside town, Cold Sands. On the left of the stage a serving table, a screen and one laid restaurant table, together with a sign on which a lugubrious-looking stag is painted, represent the serving room and part of the dining room of the 'Stag at Bay' hotel. Stage right a desk, a telephone and two chairs represent the lawyer's office.

The three areas are not lit at the same time. The action is divided between them.

As the curtain rises the back area is faintly lit. Somewhere a barrel organ is playing 'Home Sweet Home'.

The lights fade on the background and the hotel side of the stage is lit to discover FRUTE, *a small, unhappy, middle aged man, dressed as a waiter, standing with four soup plates precariously balanced up one arm.* MRS MORGAN, *a pleasant-looking woman in her thirties, is watching him anxiously.*

The plates crash to the ground. MRS MORGAN *stoops to pick up the pieces.* FRUTE *looks ruefully down at the wreckage.*

FRUTE. Careless again!

MRS MORGAN. Let me help.

FRUTE (*too discouraged to help her*). I feel I shall never master it. . . .

MRS MORGAN. What, Mr Frute?

FRUTE. The trick waiters are supposed to have. When four plates lie up that arm and another spins in the hand like Chinese juggling.

MRS MORGAN. Come now, Mr Frute, it's not so hard. When you've been a waiter so long. . . .

FRUTE. Not so long as you think, Mrs Morgan. You, you're so skilful. Have you been, many years, a waitress?

MRS MORGAN. Fifteen. I think it makes fifteen.

FRUTE. A good stint.

MRS MORGAN. The feet suffer.

FRUTE. They do. That's just it. I long for a sit down.

MRS MORGAN. Isn't the dining room empty by now?

FRUTE. Almost.

MRS MORGAN. Let's have a look see. (*She peers into the darkness on the other side of the screen.*) The honeymooners have just come in. They've been on the prom and they're *soaking*!

FRUTE. I don't feel up to the honeymooners tonight. Shall I . . . ?

MRS MORGAN. Yes?

FRUTE. Shall I tell them it's all off, except the cold?

MRS MORGAN. You could. But would it be kind? They're in love.

FRUTE. Oblivious, might we hope, to what they're tasting?

MRS MORGAN. We only honeymoon it once, Mr Frute.

FRUTE. Well, some of us.

MRS MORGAN. And in love, I feel sure, they'd fancy something hot.

FRUTE. I must soldier on?

MRS MORGAN. No, you have a little rest. I'll get the order.

> MRS MORGAN *exits.* FRUTE, *sitting on the serving table, brings out a notebook and pencil and begins, laboriously, to write.* MRS MORGAN *comes bustling back.*

That's alright, dear. They've ordered.

> MRS MORGAN *shouts to an unseen cook off stage.* FRUTE *is still making notes.*

MRS MORGAN. Gladys!

GLADYS (*off*). Aw Ug Ug Ug.

MRS MORGAN. Two brown windsors. Two steak pies. Cabbage and chips.

GLADYS (*off*). 'Ips off.

MRS MORGAN. Make it boiled then, dear. There now, some-thing nice and hot for them.

She turns round and sees FRUTE *taking notes.*

You been writing again, Mr Frute?

FRUTE (*embarrassed, he shuts his notebook*). Just . . . something to write up.

MRS MORGAN. You do write a lot, don't you? Big family to keep up with, I expect.

FRUTE. No family at all, Mrs Morgan.

MRS MORGAN. Business, then?

FRUTE. Purely business.

GLADYS (*off*). Two ownzizzors.

MRS MORGAN. Gladys *is* slippy tonight. Mind the lift, dear.

Crash of lift, off stage. MRS MORGAN *exits. Returns with two plates of soup.*

There, she always gets the rims all sloshy. . . .

FRUTE. Shall I take it?

MRS MORGAN. No, you sit and rest. Give you a chance to finish up your writing. Besides, the windsor stains so if you do have a spill.

MRS MORGAN *disappears into the darkness on the other side of the screen. While she is gone,* FRUTE *writes again. He is swearing at a broken pencil as she returns.*

FRUTE. Damn.

MRS MORGAN. Something happened?

FRUTE. I've broken my pencil, the one and only.

MRS MORGAN. Here, borrow my indelible.

FRUTE. That's kind.

MRS MORGAN. Don't suck it, now. I often do that when the figures baffle. Then a tea or a hot dinner will stare up, and me not realizing I'm frothing all purple at the mouth, epilep-tic. . . .

He goes on writing as she says:

Really, those honeymooners. He wants wine.

FRUTE (*looking up*). Wine, Mrs Morgan?

MRS MORGAN. I told him we only had the Graves or the Bones –

FRUTE. What's he want with wine?

MRS MORGAN. To add a bit of colour to life, perhaps.

FRUTE. If you try to add colour to life it only ends, in my business experience, in the payment of high legal costs.

MRS MORGAN. Better humour him. I'll get it.

> MRS MORGAN *exits.* FRUTE *begins to speak as he laboriously writes. He uses the more stilted, classier voice in which, as a private detective, he gives evidence in court.*

FRUTE (*confidentially*). In re Captain Morgan's divorce: your observer Frute takes the liberty to report. It was no doubt fortunate from the point of view of keeping a close watch on Mrs Morgan, that your observer was able to obtain the post of temporary waiter at the Stag at Bay Hotel, Cold Sands. However, your observer is not finding the art of waiting even in a temporary capacity, an altogether easy one to master. Neither is it always convenient to combine prompt attention in the dining-room with the many and intricate duties expected of a skilled Private Detective. . . .

> FRUTE *hears something. Then tiptoes off, writing, to investigate. Fade out light on serving room.*

> *The lawyer's office is illuminated. The* LAWYER *and the* CAPTAIN *have entered and taken their seats at the desk during* FRUTE'S *last speech.*

> *The* LAWYER *is reading from* FRUTE'S *report.*

LAWYER. 'Be that as it may, your observer has at present formed the opinion that Mrs Morgan is leading a life of so-called innocence.' (*He puts down the report.*) Well, Captain Morgan. That's Frute's first report on your wife. Nothing sensational as yet, but useful spadework, do admit. Very useful spadework.

CAPT. MORGAN. It's pretty distasteful.

LAWYER. Of course.

CAPT. MORGAN. When I married I only asked for a little love, a touch of infatuation. I was young. You may find it hard to credit.

LAWYER. On the contrary, Captain Morgan. I assume you have been quite young, in your time.

CAPT. MORGAN. It was natural to expect her to be devoted. A normal woman would have been blindly devoted. I gave her the earth.

LAWYER (*turning over a file*). Yours is a very slim file for a matrimonial, but let that pass. No years of nagging, no decades of sullen silence here. Three hundred and forty-two, no a miscast, three hundred and forty-one, if my mathematics serve me, days, and naturally, it must follow, nights, of married life. Then your wife demands a separation. You didn't argue?

CAPT. MORGAN. One has a certain pride.

LAWYER. Understood. So you signed the Separation Agreement for – was it five shillings a week?

CAPT. MORGAN. Seven and six.

LAWYER. Indeed! But it's not paid as she . . . vanishes. Then, from a clear sky, we get the postcard of last March. Postmark Cold Sands. Simply states your wife's hand is childishly legible, 'Hope you are well, Edna'. We set our man Frute on to her and she's gone to ground as a waitress at the Stag at Bay Hotel. Now, you're anxious to shed her without delay?

CAPT. MORGAN. No desperate hurry.

LAWYER. To my other clients marriage is the great, heavy eiderdown to be kicked off in the hot middle of the night.

CAPT. MORGAN. If she could have been made to see it straight, she'd have loved me.

LAWYER (*reassuringly*). Not a doubt.

CAPT. MORGAN. Her mother should have *spoken* to her.

LAWYER. Parents are so silent.

CAPT. MORGAN. What could have been *wrong* with me?

LAWYER. Nothing, I feel sure.

CAPT. MORGAN. I gave her everything.

LAWYER. Indeed, yes.

CAPT. MORGAN (*a burst of confidence*). One doesn't boast about the commissioned rank, but I'd lived a pretty clean life. Doctor checked me when I had marriage in view. That was only fair. Saturdays with the Richmond Cross Country Run was a habit of mine. As far as fitness went I was top-notch by the wedding breakfast. There was money in the bank, a house on mortgage and a serviceable roadster. Was there anything a normal woman wouldn't have loved?

LAWYER. I can think of nothing at the moment.

CAPT. MORGAN. And when I picked her out. . . .

LAWYER. Let me see, before she married you she was. . . .

CAPT. MORGAN. It's pretty sordid.

LAWYER. Her job of work?

CAPT. MORGAN. No, I mean the divorce. A private detective. The Law Court crammed with doubtful women in black dresses and men with co-respondent's shoes. The headlines, '*Captain's wife antics in seaside hotel*'. I may have been a bit of a romantic in my younger days. Running along Richmond Park, chasing the little, bright scraps of paper, my thoughts often turned to love and marriage. I got a different picture, then, of how it was all going to be.

LAWYER. Be of good heart, Captain Morgan. The divorce will be quite simple. All we need is a touch of evidence. Has love, for instance, beckoned to Mrs Morgan? I mean since she parted from your good self.

CAPT. MORGAN. Love? With her it doesn't enter in.

LAWYER. After all, she's a woman. We can count on the frailty of her sex, ably assisted by the tireless Frute. If she is addicted to love, Frute will unearth it.

CAPT. MORGAN. More than I could. Good luck to him.
LAWYER. Good luck to him, Captain Morgan? Good luck to
us all. I'll see you out.

The LAWYER *ushers the* CAPTAIN *out of his office. Fade out*
light on office.

Fade in light on serving room. FRUTE *enters. He is holding a*
vegetable dish and two spoons in one hand. He makes a scoop
at the dish and drops the spoons.

MRS. MORGAN (*off*). Mr Frute. What are you doing?
FRUTE. Trying out your expert way of serving the cabbage.

MRS MORGAN *enters and picks up the spoons and puts the*
dish on the table.

MRS MORGAN. Don't embark on it, Mr Frute, until I've had
the chance of giving you a few lessons.
FRUTE. Mrs Morgan. . . .
MRS MORGAN. Yes?
FRUTE. Am I right in thinking that you're 'off' this afternoon?
MRS MORGAN. Well, I am.
FRUTE. And doing – anything in particular?
MRS MORGAN (*pause – pleased*). Not really.
FRUTE. Meeting perhaps Mister Special?
MRS MORGAN. No one special.
FRUTE. I see. . . .
MRS MORGAN. As a matter of fact, Mr Frute, I'll tell you quite
candidly, I've been living alone so long. . . .
FRUTE. Yes. . . .
MRS MORGAN. And it's on the days off one feels it most.
FRUTE. Like me, you haven't picked up many friends?
MRS MORGAN. When you're working you forget about it, but
in the time off, it hits you. Eating alone in cafes.
FRUTE. Sitting alone in the cinema, reading the newspaper
when they turn up the lights for organ music. . . .

MRS MORGAN. No call to put on a best dress and no helpful
hand behind you to zip you in. . . .

FRUTE. And this afternoon?

MRS MORGAN. If nothing transpires I may go out with Gladys.
She's a good sort, really, when you get her on your own
level. Not shouting up that lift. . . .

FRUTE. If you're really fixed up with Gladys. . . .

MRS MORGAN. We've nothing firm.

FRUTE. You may . . . meet someone else?

MRS MORGAN. I mean if you, Mr Frute. . . .

FRUTE. Oh Mrs Morgan. I'm afraid that would not be possible.

MRS MORGAN. You're busy?

FRUTE. It wouldn't be (*grandly*) professional etiquette.

MRS MORGAN (*mystified*). I suppose not. . . . Well, I'll be seeing
you.

FRUTE. I don't think so. But I, Mrs Morgan, shall be seeing
you. Oh, Mrs Morgan. . . .

MRS MORGAN. Yes?

FRUTE. Before you go?

MRS MORGAN (*hopefully*). Yes, Mr Frute?

FRUTE. Might I ask. . . .

MRS MORGAN. Of course.

FRUTE. For the further loan of the pencil.

MRS MORGAN (*disappointed*). Well, here it is.

> *She goes, and* FRUTE *begins to write. As he writes he speaks.*

FRUTE. Mrs Morgan is about to embark on her period of
'Time Off'. This is the period when she is most likely to
indulge in marital infidelity if she be so minded. Your
observer Frute proposes to keep in constant, but discreet
attendance. . . .

> FRUTE *gets his hat and exits after* MRS MORGAN. MRS
> MORGAN *and* GLADYS *appear backstage by the railings and
> the shelter.* FRUTE *enters and speaks confidentially to the
> audience.*

FRUTE. . . . Mrs Morgan appears to be spending the time off
    with Gladys from the kitchen. This is a strange choice
    having regard to the fact that Mrs Morgan is such a hand-
    some, indeed an attractive individual.

    MRS MORGAN *and* GLADYS *turn up the collars of their*
    mackintoshes as they walk.

Weather conditions for keeping observation are not ideal.
    There is a distinct fog from the North Sea. Winters at Cold
    Sands are said to be severe. They could hardly be more
    severe than the summers. . . . However, you may rest
    assured that climatic conditions will in no way deter your
    observer Frute. . . .

    They are by the shelter.

MRS MORGAN. It's coming down torrential again. Slip into the
    shelter, shall we?
GLADYS. Mmmmmm.

    They sit in the shelter. FRUTE *crosses furtively and sits on a*
    seat behind them. He peers at them and writes.

MRS MORGAN. It's not often you get drawn to another human
    being, is it, Gladys? But this Mr Frute is so nicely spoken,
    and a child when it comes to plates. . . .
GLADYS. Yerrum.
MRS MORGAN. And he's got such a sensitive look. I never
    remember such a fine-drawn appearance on any man. But
    when I was quite young we took in a lodger, ever such a
    gentle, sensitive type of man, and once I burst into his
    bedroom unbeknownst and he was saying his prayers. He
    really was. Kneeling by his bed, and I saw that hole shining
    pink in the sole of his sock and I thought poor fellow, and I
    felt so sorry for him, as when this Mr Frute breaks a plate. . . .
GLADYS. Deeyerrr.
MRS MORGAN. Well, I was telling you about this fellow with

H

the hole in his sock. So fine-drawn he was, and one day the
police came for him and they removed him from us and it
seemed that he had not two wives but five, and very nice
types of women and all in different parts of England, the
Channel Islands and the Isle of Man. Not that our waiter, of
course. . . . Sometimes I wonder if he *is* a waiter. What if
he were doing it all for some *woman*. . . . But that's nonsense
like you read in those weekly books. . . .

GLADYS. Nummmmm.

MRS MORGAN. No offence, Gladys dear, but you're not a great
one for conversation, are you?

FRUTE (*speaking as he writes*). Your observer can only describe
this as a summer blizzard. (*Sneezes.*) There are distinct
traces of hail. (*He peers out to sea.*) There seems to be some
distress at sea. The Cold Sands lifeboat is apparently being
launched. From the few sentences which I could hear, it
seemed that Mrs Morgan was discussing some man for whom
she felt a decided glow of affection. In the roar of the summer
blizzard your observer was unable to hear the name of the
said individual. . . .

MRS MORGAN. Come on then, Gladys. We'll miss the
picture. . . .

   *They get up and we see them walk down to the railings to
   exit.* FRUTE *exits, following them. Slowly all the lights fade.
   When they come on again* FRUTE *is sitting in the serving
   room writing.*

FRUTE (*speaking as he writes*). Without any opportunity to
change into dry clothing, your observer followed Mrs
Morgan to the Pix Picture Palace in High Street where a
lengthy 'Double Feature' programme was viewed. Halfway
through the Newsreel, Mrs Morgan was addressed by a
strange man in the two-and-three's. Mrs Morgan at once,
with some delicacy and financial sacrifice, changed her seat
and that of Gladys to the one-and-nines. Your observer is
not of the opinion that this man was in any way connected

with the individual of whom Mrs Morgan had spoken with warmth and affection. (*Cough.*) Your observer intends, with redoubled vigilance, to keep watch on all of Mrs Morgan's activities. (*Burst of coughs and sneezes.*) Despite his at present, extremely heavy cold. . . .

> *Fade out light on serving room.* FRUTE *exits. Fade in on lawyer's office. The* LAWYER *and* CAPTAIN *enter and take their seats.*

LAWYER. It appears our observer has a heavy cold.

CAPT. MORGAN (*anxious*). He won't crock up?

LAWYER. Frute will soldier on. He is a little terrier after an affair of the heart. And doesn't it seem we've struck oil?

CAPT. MORGAN. Oil?

LAWYER. Talking, you see, of another man.

CAPT. MORGAN (*pause, then very excited*). Of course. There must be another man. He's the answer to the problem that's tortured me all these years.

LAWYER. This . . .

CAPT. MORGAN. Enticer. This C.3. rat. This thin, brown foreigner with his big car and his Golders Green Wholesale Grocery and his long black oily sideboards. . . .

LAWYER. Furniture?

CAPT. MORGAN. Hair.

LAWYER. You know him?

CAPT. MORGAN. Of course not.

LAWYER. But?

CAPT. MORGAN. He's the missing link. She loved me. But he mesmerized her. Now, poor girl, she wants to come creeping back.

LAWYER. You'd have her?

CAPT. MORGAN. No. Pride.

LAWYER. Ah!

CAPT. MORGAN. Of course he's got the power of his bank

balance. Even though he's bald and fat and red-eyes and calls his sitting-room the lounge.

LAWYER. But I thought you described. . . .

CAPT. MORGAN. We don't know him exactly yet. We only know he *must* exist.

LAWYER. Can we go quite so far? The report merely says that a man was mentioned.

CAPT. MORGAN. But she left me. Any Court would draw the inference.

LAWYER. I fear not. After all, it may have been an innocent ...

CAPT. MORGAN. Innocent! You're a lawyer, you don't believe that?

LAWYER. My dear Captain, as a lawyer I believe nothing. My mind is a lean, well-dieted stomach, only capable of taking in that which can satisfy it beyond reasonable doubt. And yet I know that out of the ten persons with whom I travel daily in the train, one must be an adulterer, another a bigamist, a third a slanderer of goods and so on. If it were not so, these offences, in all their legal profusion, would not exist. I see no reason why your wife should be different from the rest of humanity. But at present, I fear, I smell no odour of proof.

CAPT. MORGAN. It'll come. If Frute only sticks to her.

LAWYER. He'll stick to her, Captain Morgan. Like a leech. . . .

Fade out light on lawyer's office as LAWYER *exits, showing the* CAPTAIN *to the door.*

Fade in light on serving room. FRUTE *is trying to speak to* GLADYS. *Obviously he is having no success and she exits. He sits down to write, speaking as he does so.*

FRUTE. In the days that have passed since Mrs Morgan's 'time off' there has been no further sign of the individual of whom she was heard to confide. Your observer has attempted to elicit the name of this individual from the female Gladys, but the said Gladys is of the 'strong and silent' variety, and

your observer was reluctant to let the 'cat out of the bag' by
pressing his enquiries 'home'.

> FRUTE *has a fit of coughing as* MRS MORGAN *enters. He
> puts his notebook away guiltily.*

MRS MORGAN. The trouble is you're not really fit for work
with that terrible cold on you. We saw you the other night,
Gladys and I.

FRUTE (*sneeze*). Did you, Mrs Morgan?

MRS MORGAN. We saw you in the cinema. We waved, but
you didn't pay all that attention. You looked a bit miserable as I remarked to Gladys, as if you were in your wet
clothes.

FRUTE. Mrs Morgan, to be frank with you, so I was.

MRS MORGAN. Enjoy your 'time off' did you?

FRUTE. Not specially.

MRS MORGAN. On the front were you?

FRUTE. Yes. Did you see the wreck?

MRS MORGAN. What wreck?

FRUTE. They launched the lifeboat.

MRS MORGAN. Bless you, that wasn't the lifeboat!

FRUTE. Those grim-faced men in oil skins?

MRS MORGAN. Holiday-makers. That was the pleasure trip,
from the end of the pier. And you thought there'd been a
catastrophe. . . . (*Laughs.*)

FRUTE (*laughing with her*). A sinking at the least.

MRS MORGAN (*laughing*). And suppose if you'd dived in to save
a life!

FRUTE (*laughing, then serious*). Well, hardly Mrs Morgan, I
breast stroke it a few yards. Not exactly up to Cross Channel
standard.

MRS MORGAN (*very serious*). But I'm sure you'd have had a try,
if anyone was in distress.

FRUTE (*flattered*). Well, a stab at it perhaps.

MRS MORGAN. There now, you see.

Pause.

FRUTE. Mrs Morgan, since I have been working here I will say you've shown me every kindness. I regard you, if I may say so, without offence, as a sincerely helpful type of individual. . . .

MRS MORGAN. Go along. . . .

FRUTE. Always ready, as you've shown many a time when a plate slipped or I got the Golden Roll in ahead of the Brown Windsor, to rescue a fellow being.

MRS MORGAN. What about you, Mr Frute? The way you stood poised on that pier, ready to dive off when you thought there'd been a wrecking . . .

FRUTE. Not quite poised perhaps. But to return to you. . . .

MRS MORGAN. Soaked to the skin. Scanning that sea for survivors. . . .

FRUTE. What I'm leading to, Mrs Morgan, is that, only you can help one if it isn't a liberty.

MRS MORGAN. Anything, Mr Frute.

FRUTE. It's a business matter. It's not going too smoothly as it so happens. . . .

MRS MORGAN. I'm sorry. . . .

FRUTE. I don't like to approach you directly like this.

MRS MORGAN. Whatever can it be?

FRUTE. Well then, not to make a meal, rumour has it. . . .

MRS MORGAN. Rumour?

FRUTE. That there may be a gentleman in whom you are especially interested.

MRS MORGAN. Don't be so silly, Mr Frute. There's only ever been one man in my life, and just my luck we didn't hit it.

FRUTE. The Captain?

MRS MORGAN. How did you know?

FRUTE. Rumour.

MRS MORGAN. Has it, I suppose.

FRUTE. Exactly, yes. You didn't hit it apparently.

MRS MORGAN. We met in the early war years. 'Marry me,' he said, 'I shall soon be sent abroad and killed.'

FRUTE. Sound reason.

MRS MORGAN. It didn't work out like that. They put him in charge of an Army Post Office at Pullborough. He got a sleeping-out pass every night.

FRUTE. What led you two to matrimony?

MRS MORGAN. Loneliness perhaps. My mother and father had passed. I was working in the West End of London.

FRUTE. Shop assistant?

MRS MORGAN. Cigarette kiosk on Platform 9 at Paddington. The Captain made the journey regular. I knew nothing about him really, and of me he only knew what he saw.

FRUTE. Which was. . . .

MRS MORGAN. The head and shoulders. A kiosk doesn't give all that away. Afterwards he blamed that kiosk, and as he used to say, it was the mix up of social classes due to the war that led him on to marry me –

FRUTE. Socially conscious?

MRS MORGAN. That I didn't resent, but such a jumpy nervous type of man. Thank God, he'd say, I'll always keep one bullet in this revolver for you. . . .

FRUTE. Why on earth?

MRS MORGAN. In case the war picture changed, and I got raped by the Russians. . . . I couldn't see it his way. Let's meet that little trouble, I told him often enough, when it comes. Then he got so over-excited. He took it in his head that I'd only married him for his little black saloon car. We hadn't any petrol for it anyway. So he gave that little car to a brother officer. Then he said that I'd only married him because of the handsome gold watch I'd spotted on his wrist. So he smashed that with a heavy hammer and shouted out 'Now love me for myself alone.' Or he'd run out of the bathroom, even his dark horn rims left off. 'This is the man' he'd cry out, 'stripped of his regimentals – can't you love me

for what I am?' Put like that, Mr Frute, and I just couldn't.
I told him so, so he gave me the Separation Agreement. 'A
gentleman can't turn you off with nothing,' he said, as he
signed for that seven and six a week. Never kept it up, of
course.

FRUTE. Ungenerous?

MRS MORGAN. Always suspicious – always wanting to be
loved. And always taking little lumps of coal off the fire
because he said I'd only married him for the extra fuel
allotment. One year's married life and I've never been so
cold. Then he'd shout, 'I'm extremely popular, I'm well
liked at Pullborough. Why can't you be the same as everyone
else? Love me, damn you.' Well, I didn't and that was that.
It wasn't a home like I remembered.

FRUTE. Which was that?

MRS MORGAN. Dalston Junction. My father's place.

FRUTE. They can be comfortable round there.

MRS MORGAN. Small and compact. Nothing big about it.

FRUTE. But. . . .

MRS MORGAN. Warm. You'd come back from school or
shopping with a wind cutting your face and your fingers stiff
as chicken claws, and to open that door – it was like a kiss of
air from the underground.

FRUTE. That. . . .

MRS MORGAN. Was what I appreciated. A welcome to unfreeze
your face. Father, he'd come home every Friday and out he'd
spread his whole wage packet on the oil-cloth. He didn't ask
to be loved just for himself. A different class of man entirely.

FRUITE. So you left . . . the Captain?

MRS MORGAN. I didn't think he ever saw the point.

FRUTE. And since that day. There's been no one?

MRS MORGAN. If I'd met a man who didn't expect anyone to
like him. . . .

FRUTE. You never have?

MRS MORGAN. No. And *your* home?

FRUTE. Run by the Essex County Council. Between eight and nine hundred of us. A big family like that, the superintendent always explained, rubs the edges off you.

MRS MORGAN. I'm sorry. But matrimony has never – appealed?

FRUTE. Never come my way, in *private* life, that is. Too late now, we really must assume.

MRS MORGAN. Well, Mr Frute.

FRUTE. Yes, Mrs Morgan?

MRS MORGAN. We seem to be two of a kind.

Pause.

Another lunch time.

FRUTE (*slapping his pocket*). I'm clean out of smokes.

MRS MORGAN. Slip out for a few if you'd care to. I'll polish these up.

FRUTE. I'm leaving all the work to you. . . .

MRS MORGAN. Go on. Do you good to get a breath of air that didn't smell of soup.

FRUTE. I won't be many minutes. . . . (*He goes out.*)

MRS MORGAN *breathes on a glass, sings and polishes.*

MRS MORGAN (*singing*).
　　　　'Mid pleasures and palaces
　　　　Long may we roam.
　　　　We always come back for . . .
　　　　There's no place like home.'
She exits singing.

Fade in back stage.

A man is sitting reading a newspaper in the shelter. He lowers his newspaper as FRUTE *enters and passes him. He is revealed as* CAPTAIN MORGAN.

CAPT. MORGAN. Here. What's your name? Frute?

FRUTE *stops, bewildered.*

FRUTE. Whoever . . .

CAPT. MORGAN. I'm Captain Morgan.

FRUTE. Really, this is very distressing. . . .

CAPT. MORGAN. For *you*?

FRUTE. It's not etiquette. A direct approach from the client.
It's not professional. A gentleman never bandies words with
his detective. A gentleman speaks to his solicitor who speaks
to me, his detective, upon the telephone. Oh dear, this is
very unknown.

CAPT. MORGAN. It's hardly pleasant for me. I need your
reassurance.

FRUTE. You need . . . ?

CAPT. MORGAN. Look here. When I spotted you I assumed
you were following my wife.

FRUTE. No. As a matter of fact. . . .

CAPT. MORGAN. What?

FRUTE (*lamely*). Just slipped out for a packet of smokes.

CAPT. MORGAN. Really?

FRUTE. Now, don't worry. At the moment she's laying up the
lunch and I'm on my way back to . . . help her. She can't
escape.

CAPT. MORGAN. And the other scoundrel. You have a finger
on him?

FRUTE. Who?

CAPT. MORGAN. The frightful R.A.F. salesman outsider with
his spotted scarf and his walrus whiskers and his, 'Down the
hatch, here's to the Good Old Duke' in the saloon bar until
half an hour past closing time. . . .

FRUTE. I've no idea where *he* is.

CAPT. MORGAN. You've lost him?

FRUTE. Never found him.

CAPT. MORGAN. Don't torment me, I beg of you. What are
you trying to blurt out?

FRUTE. Up till now, no other man has put in an appearance.

CAPT. MORGAN. Up till now . . . ?

FRUTE. Your wife, and my observations but confirm the opinion I first formed of her, appears to be an honest and indeed an innocent woman.

Pause.

CAPT. MORGAN (*horrified*). How can that be possible?

FRUTE. They exist.

CAPT. MORGAN. But she . . . she wanted the separation. She broke up our marriage.

FRUTE. Some time ago.

CAPT. MORGAN. Nothing very innocent about that.

FRUTE. There may have been no . . . other man.

Pause.

CAPT. MORGAN (*incredulous*). You're not suggesting – that she simply took a dislike to me. . . .

FRUTE. One wouldn't credit it.

CAPT. MORGAN. But I'm well liked. Even some women have rather liked me.

FRUTE. Well, now. . . .

CAPT. MORGAN. Look me steadily in the eye. What could she have found not to love about me? Great Scott, it's not logical. There must have been a seducer.

FRUTE. That's our hope.

CAPT. MORGAN. You do give me then, that small glimmer of hope?

FRUTE. If we continue our investigations. . . .

CAPT. MORGAN. Continue them please. Continue them like a good little fellow.

FRUTE. You'll permit a word of advice?

CAPT. MORGAN. Yes.

FRUTE. Take a train. First class as your rank is entitled. Go home. Leave this job to the experts. All that the human eye can see of your wife is under observation.

FRUTE *exits.*

CAPT. MORGAN. Very well . . . I'll take your advice . . . news
of her infidelity would be a great comfort. . . . (*His voice trails
off as he shouts after* FRUTE.)

Fade out.

When the lights fade in the LAWYER *is finishing a meal at
the dining table.* MRS MORGAN *has just finished waiting on
him.* FRUTE *enters the serving room behind the screen.*

LAWYER. No doubt you are competent at your work, madam,
and you may call it anti-feminism, but I want the waiter to
bring me my bill.

MRS MORGAN *shrugs her shoulders and goes behind the screen
into the serving room. There,* FRUTE *is singing to himself.*

FRUTE (*singing*).
　　　　　'We always come back for . . .
　　　　　There's no place like home'. . . .

MRS MORGAN. You sound happy. Business going well?

FRUTE. There comes a time, Mrs Morgan, in any business,
when you have to control the customer – and when it comes
there's a battle of wills, a moment of courage and puff – you
get what you want. And all without stooping to a single
untruth – a touch of deception.

MRS MORGAN. There's a gentleman alone in there. He says he
wants the waiter to bring him his bill.

FRUTE. A gentleman?

He peers through the screen then says aghast:

Mrs Morgan, I think I'm off.

LAWYER. Waiter!

MRS MORGAN. Too late. He's spied you. . . .

LAWYER. Waiter!

FRUTE (*faintly*). Coming, coming at once, sir.

FRUTE *goes round the screen and stands by the dining table.*
MRS MORGAN *exits.*

LAWYER. Well, Frute. It appears that I have winkled you out
at last.

FRUTE. We can't talk here, sir – if I may suggest. (*He writes the
bill hurriedly and puts it on the table.*)

LAWYER. I will be brief, while the lady in question is out of
the room. For me, you must realize, this is but one of a
thousand cases.

FRUTE. Of course. I realize that, sir.

LAWYER. Good. Now listen to me, Frute.

FRUTE. Yes, sir.

LAWYER. This case is not going well.

FRUTE. No, sir.

LAWYER. The client is not satisfied.

FRUTE. I realize that . . . very painful for him.

LAWYER. And painful for you, Frute.

FRUTE. Yes, sir.

LAWYER. Now time is money, and you have wasted enough of
both. I have backed you so far – now I expect results – I
expect some tangible fact to emerge. . . .

FRUTE. But sir – how can it?

LAWYER. I know nothing of your methods of going to
work.

FRUTE. No, sir.

LAWYER. Nor do I want to know. We trained men, professional
men, have our code, Frute. We have our ethics. Within the
strict frame of proper conduct we have woven the beautiful
patterns of law. You are outside all that –

FRUTE (*humbly*). Yes, sir.

LAWYER. You, Frute, have passed no examination. You have
won no fine-engraved certificates – not only are you beyond
reach of professional qualifications, honourable standards
or disciplinary bodies, you are even remote from any normal

test of human decency. What honourable man, I ask you, would invite a private detective to take tea with his wife or play with his children? The absurdity of the idea strikes you at once, does it not?

FRUTE. I suppose it does.

LAWYER. Very well, Frute. What you do, how you go about your calling is happily no concern of mine. Only don't attempt to impose on your repulsive trade the standards which are the monopoly of the decently employed citizen. You have no right to do that, Frute.

FRUTE. I suppose not, sir.

LAWYER. Bear that well in mind. And if I don't get a result in this case I shall feel unable to recommend you in future. I don't imagine, at your age, you feel particularly suited for other work? I don't fancy they'd keep you on as a waiter if I told. . . .

FRUTE. I understand. . . .

LAWYER. Very good. Let there be no unpleasantness. I do not care for unpleasantness. In your own line you may still be a success. But remember, I impress on you, what your particular line has to be. There *is* a pale, Frute, and *you* are beyond it.

The LAWYER *leaves money for the bill and exits.* FRUTE *goes back into the serving room, sits on the table and mops his brow.* MRS MORGAN *enters to him.*

MRS MORGAN (*solicitous*). Mr Frute, you look quite ill.

Pause while FRUTE *gasps and gulps.*

What is it, have you been trying to do too much?

FRUTE. Perhaps that's what it is.

MRS MORGAN. Cheer up. 'Time off' again on Thursday.

FRUTE. Time off?

MRS MORGAN. Makes a change for us, anyway.

FRUTE. You won't be . . . meeting anyone?

MRS MORGAN (*patiently*). No, Mr Frute. You know that, now
don't you?

FRUTE. Yes, I know. (*Pause.*) Probably you won't even speak
to another man?

MRS MORGAN. Probably not.

FRUTE. Let alone have tea with one.

MRS MORGAN. No. . . .

FRUTE. Or talk in an animated manner. . . .

MRS MORGAN. Not with Gladys.

FRUTE. Or be spotted arm in arm on the promenade.

MRS MORGAN (*laughing slightly*). Certainly not.

FRUTE. Then it's hopeless.

MRS MORGAN. Unlikely.

FRUTE. Unless. . . .

Pause.

MRS MORGAN. What did you say?

FRUTE. Unless. You would consider . . . you would allow. . . .

MRS MORGAN. Allow?

FRUTE. Allow me to be your escort for the 'time off'?

MRS MORGAN. Oh, Mr Frute. What a long time it's taken you
to ask.

They exit together. The lights fade.

Fade in background. MRS MORGAN *and* FRUTE *enter in
their hats and coats and stand looking out at the beach. There
is a sound of distant children's voices singing :*

'Eternal father, strong to save,
Whose hand doth bound the restless waves,
Who bidst the mighty ocean deep. . . .'

MRS MORGAN. The children's service, on the beach.

FRUTE. I can see now. There's a harmonium on the wet sand.

MRS MORGAN. The Salvation Army organize it. Something to
keep the kiddies warm.

FRUTE. On a summer holiday – not very festive. . . .

MRS MORGAN (*singing*). 'For those in peril *on* the sea.'

FRUTE. What's that?

MRS MORGAN. I was just thinking. . . .

FRUTE. What?

MRS MORGAN. That day – when you thought there was peril at sea, remember – and how quick you were to get out on the pier, to strip off. . . .

FRUTE. No, Mrs Morgan. I'm no hero. All the same I hope you'll remember me kindly. When I move on.

They go to the shelter and sit down.

MRS MORGAN. You're leaving us? Nothing wrong?

FRUTE. Purely business.

MRS MORGAN. Oh. I'm sorry.

FRUTE. I'm sorry too, Mrs Morgan.

MRS MORGAN. Waitering for you's only a sideline, isn't it, really?

FRUTE. That – is so.

MRS MORGAN. What's this other business of yours – I mean the one where you control the customer?

FRUTE. Alas, Mrs Morgan, I don't control him any more.

MRS MORGAN. But what is that business exactly?

FRUTE. Private. . . .

MRS MORGAN. Oh well. I never meant to butt in.

FRUTE. A confidential. . . .

MRS MORGAN. I quite understand. Really, you know the old 'Stag at Bay' won't seem the same without you.

FRUTE. Won't it, Mrs Morgan?

MRS MORGAN. It never seemed exactly a homely place, not before you came.

FRUTE. Not?

MRS MORGAN. But now, when I look around it, I fall to imagining. I mean, suppose that Stag at Bay were our home. It's a dream. . . .

FRUTE. A bit of a nightmare. (*Laughing.*)

MRS MORGAN. You're laughing. I may be stupid. But you and I, Mr Frute, we've no other home – so if I sometimes think, that was ours. . . .

FRUTE. Ours, Mrs Morgan?

MRS MORGAN (*almost chanting*). The twenty bottles of sauce on the tables – our bottles of sauce, the twenty cruets – our cruets. All those antlers – our antlers. And the visitors and staff – all our friends and relations.

FRUTE. Even Gladys?

MRS MORGAN. Poor Gladys. She's a decent sort really.

FRUTE. Yes. A decent sort.

Pause.

MRS MORGAN. It's a funny thing. All these years and I had no one to send a postcard to. Once I even bought a postcard and sent it to *him*, I was that lonely.

FRUTE. To *him*?

MRS MORGAN. The Captain. Now that showed I was feeling a lack.

FRUTE. What happened?

MRS MORGAN. Oh, he never even answered it. Took no notice, really.

FRUTE. You can't be sure. It may have meant a lot to him.

MRS MORGAN. I doubt that. (*Chanting again.*) The palm tree in the lounge, our palm tree.

FRUTE. It's no good going on, Mrs Morgan. I just don't fit into the pattern of family life.

MRS MORGAN. Not fit in?

FRUTE. I'm outside it somehow. I've had it all explained. . . .

MRS MORGAN. Whatever can you mean?

FRUTE. You may find it difficult to understand.

MRS MORGAN. Yes.

FRUTE. But what I'm doing for you – well I only hope it will make you feel more free, when. . . .

I

MRS MORGAN. 'When'. . . .

FRUTE (*with a rush*). When a man of decent qualifications does come along – as we hope and believe he must.

Pause.

MRS MORGAN. After you're gone . . . I can send you a postcard?

FRUTE. Certainly Mrs Morgan – and to tell you the truth. . . . I'm really glad it was me you went out with today. I shouldn't have liked it to have been anyone else, not today, know what I mean?

MRS MORGAN. Can't say I do.

FRUTE. Time will show, Mrs Morgan. It is, I want you to understand, just my peculiar line.

MRS MORGAN. I'm sure you mean no harm.

FRUTE. I don't, really I don't.

MRS MORGAN. Come on then, we'll miss the picture. I must say it'll be nice having someone to talk to in the pictures, when they play the organ and the lights go up and all the couples round you are caught so friendly.

FRUTE. It makes a difference, having someone to talk to.

MRS MORGAN. The pictures don't drag so. Come on. We'll miss the love picture. Do you like love pictures, Mr Frute?

FRUTE. Up to now I've always preferred detection. Of course, detective work. . . .

MRS MORGAN. Yes?

FRUTE. It's more concerned with love than many people might think. . . .

The lights fade as they exit together. Cinema organ music is heard for a moment, then the lights fade in on serving room.

MRS MORGAN *and* MR FRUTE *come in in their outdoor coats.*

MRS MORGAN (*yawns*). Best 'time off' I ever had.

FRUTE. Me too.

MRS MORGAN. I'm climbing up to the home from home.

FRUTE. Which is?

MRS MORGAN. Room 51. Right up the stairs. Just next door to the water tank. You must be tired.

FRUTE. Not really. And I've still a little writing to do.

MRS MORGAN. Get you something?

FRUTE. No thanks. And thank you, Mrs Morgan – thank you for everything.

Pause. As she goes.

MRS MORGAN. Don't work too hard at that old writing now. . . .

She gives him a lingering, solicitous look and goes out of the door. FRUTE *sits down at the serving table, takes out his notebook and pencil, and begins to wrestle with his conscience.*

FRUTE (*sighs. Pauses. Whistles the first bar of 'No Place Like Home' sighs again*). What did he say? No professional standards. No disciplinary bodies. No normal test of human decency. . . . Beyond the pale . . . (*sighs*). He's right, Frute. You know he's right. (*sighs.*) It's a useful job after all. After all, someone's got to do it. After all, we can't all choose. (*determined.*) Go on Frute, put pencil to paper. (*regretful.*) Oh, you never gave her back her pencil. . . . (*whispering.*) Get on with it, man, and – make it lively reading. . . . Make it artistic. Write it, like you always wanted it to happen. . . .

FRUTE *exits.*

Fade in lights on lawyer's office. LAWYER *and* CAPTAIN *have entered quietly during* FRUTE'S *last speech. The* LAWYER *is just finished reading* FRUTE'S *last report.*

LAWYER. 'And after their departure from the Pix Picture Palace, where it is not suggested misconduct took place, the evening ended with the gentleman in question escorting Mrs Morgan to her "home from home" as she so phrases it,

room number 51, at the top of the stairs, next door to the
water tank.'

> *The* LAWYER *looks at* CAPTAIN MORGAN *in great and
> silent satisfaction. Then he opens a drawer of the desk, brings
> out a sherry decanter and two glasses, fills them and motions
> his client to a glass. They raise glasses solemnly to each other
> and drink.*

CAPT. MORGAN. Frute's been brilliant. Just brilliant. Quite a
  first-class brain he must have under that quaint old hat of his.
  For a moment you know, I'd misjudged him.

LAWYER. I always told you, I think, that Frute was a
  perfectly sound little worker.

CAPT. MORGAN. To pull the solution out of the bag when
  everyone has despaired of him. Bang in the tradition,
  wouldn't you agree, of the great detective brains of all time?

LAWYER. Our organization, I think, must take a little of the
  credit.

CAPT. MORGAN. Good heavens, yes. I didn't imply. . . .

LAWYER. Frute was merely content to fulfil his somewhat
  sordid function. He obeyed instructions. Few of us can do
  more.

CAPT. MORGAN. Indeed no. And now it's definite. There's
  another man. I'm safe. I feel well-liked – I feel surrounded
  with affection. Oh, the difference Frute has made to me. And
  Mrs Morgan?

LAWYER. Will receive her Divorce Petition, based on her
  matrimonial misconduct, in a sealed envelope and by A.R.
  Registered Post.

CAPT. MORGAN (*thinking*). Registered Post, eh? Serve her
  right if it is by Registered Post. Great Scott, I'd like to see
  her face when she opens that. . . . Registered Post did you
  say?

> *They have finished their drinks and the* LAWYER, *nodding,*

ushers the CAPTAIN *firmly out of the office. As they exit, fade in the light on the serving room.*

MRS MORGAN *enters with a suitcase. She puts the case down and looks round regretfully.* FRUTE *enters with his possessions in a paper parcel. They are both in outdoor clothes. They look at each other in surprise.*

MRS MORGAN. You're leaving?

FRUTE. My work's over. But you. . . .

MRS MORGAN. I had this. (*Pulls paper from her overcoat.*)

FRUTE. Oh, yes. That. . . .

MRS MORGAN. It seems I've done misconduct.

FRUTE. Well, you see. . . .

MRS MORGAN (*reading*). 'On Thursday, the 12th day of September, at the Stag at Bay Hotel, Cold Sands.' I'd better leave. I can't get the old Stag involved in that sort of thing. It's got enough to depress it already.

FRUTE. Very considerate.

MRS MORGAN (*reading*). 'With a man unknown. . . .' (*Looks up.*) Mr Frute, there was no unknown man! You were with me all the time. You can say. . . . Why, whatever's the matter . . . ?

FRUTE. Mrs Morgan, I feel ashamed. I think even I . . . even I'm entitled to feel ashamed.

MRS MORGAN. Of course you are, Mr Frute, if you really want to.

FRUTE. I feel really terrible. But there was no harm to me. When I first felt drawn to this class of work. . . .

MRS MORGAN. Poor Mr Frute. You've had a terrible shock.

FRUTE. It was only a young boy's spirit of adventure. At the home when the other boys were out playing on the asphalt, I was locked. . . . I'm boring you.

MRS MORGAN (*completely bewildered*). No, Mr Frute. You were locked apparently. . . .

FRUTE. In the lavatory by the old boiler room. Reading. How

the muffled woman came to Baker Street, how the secret
papers got into the breakfast dish. How the rose came from
Ruritania.

MRS MORGAN. Enthralled?

FRUTE. Even at that age I knew the risks I was running. I had
to be skilled with the foils, sudden with a loaded ash plant,
able to sit for long hours in silence in a darkened room and
only a mulatto breathing for company. . . .

MRS MORGAN. Sounds creepy.

FRUTE. Not woman's work, I can assure you. Then, when I
left the home I found the opening at last. I became a
private . . .

MRS MORGAN. Yes, Mr Frute?

FRUTE. Detective. And of course I became – beyond the pale –
as the expression is.

MRS MORGAN. In what way, Mr Frute?

FRUTE. Nice people, Mrs Morgan, don't know many private
detectives.

MRS MORGAN. Their loss, Mr Frute.

FRUTE. Kind of you to say so, but . . . what I'm trying to get
out is – it was in the course of my work that we . . .

MRS MORGAN. Yes?

FRUTE. Met.

MRS MORGAN. Met, Mr Frute?

FRUTE. I was employed by your husband – to keep an eye on you.

MRS MORGAN (*very quiet and thoughtful*). So you. . .

FRUTE. Yes. And I wrote the report that led to that terrible
accusation. Oh, Mrs Morgan – I took a terrible liberty with
the truth. . . .

MRS MORGAN. Yes, Mr Frute.

FRUTE. It was all – wishful thinking.

MRS MORGAN. Wishful?

FRUTE (*very agitated*). But I'll deny it all. I'll say it was all a lie.
I'll clear your name. You've been so kind. . . . Oh, Mrs
Morgan. I'll put it right.

MRS MORGAN (*thoughtful*). Mr Frute. If you don't deny it. If you go to Court and give clear oath evidence of my . . . misconduct?

FRUTE. I couldn't!

MRS MORGAN. But if you could. . . .

FRUTE. It would be a terrible deception, of the Judge, your husband, you . . . even me. . . .

MRS MORGAN. Yes. And I'd be free?

FRUTE. I expect so. Yes.

MRS MORGAN. To marry again?

FRUTE. If you wanted to.

MRS MORGAN. I do want to.

Pause.

FRUTE. To a particular gentleman?

MRS MORGAN. To a man who never expected anyone to like him. To someone such as. . . .

FRUTE. Yes?

MRS MORGAN. You, Mr Frute.

Pause.

FRUTE. I don't know what to say. . . . If you *would* consider life as Mrs Frute.

MRS MORGAN. Give that clear, oath evidence! Give them the worst of me, Mr Frute! Give them misconduct *and* adultery!

FRUTE. Mrs Morgan, I will. You're a truly remarkable woman, quite outstanding. I loved you from the moment I first had you under observation.

MRS MORGAN. And we'll be happy, Mr Frute.

FRUTE. I'll give up my profession.

MRS MORGAN. Why ever?

FRUTE. To a lady of your stamp . . . it's no doubt distasteful.

MRS MORGAN. It's not distasteful at all. It seems a very useful profession.

FRUTE. Another pair of eyes is often a help.

MRS MORGAN. I'd be proud to help, Mr Frute. And we might manage a small home?

FRUTE. No doubt of it. Shall we be off, Mrs Morgan?

MRS MORGAN. Mrs Morgan? Mrs Morgan – as was. (*Triumphantly*.) Mrs Frute, to you.

> *They leave the serving room and they are last seen walking arm in arm across the back of the stage as the Curtain slowly falls.*

Lunch Hour

First broadcast on the BBC Third Programme on 25 June, 1960, with Wendy Craig as the GIRL and Stephen Murray as the MAN. It was produced by Martyn C. Webster.

The play was first performed on the stage at the Salisbury Playhouse on 20 June, 1960, with Nancie Herrod as the GIRL and Patrick Kavanagh as the MAN. It was produced by Robert Cartland.

It was later presented by Michael Codron and David Hall at the Arts Theatre Club, London, and subsequently transferred to the Criterion Theatre, with the following cast:

(in order of appearance)

THE MAN	*Emlyn Williams*
THE GIRL	*Wendy Craig*
THE MANAGERESS	*Alison Leggatt*

Directed by Donald McWhinnie
Setting designed by Brian Currah

As the curtain rises a clock is striking one on the mantelpiece of a small hotel bedroom in the neighbourhood of King's Cross Station. It is winter.

The door is back stage, centre. Almost the only article of furniture is a large, brass-ended double bed with a white cotton cover. Otherwise the room is dingy yellow, the peeling wallpaper decorated with a recurrent pattern of castles. There is an unlit, shilling-in-the-slot gas fire, a naked electric bulb hanging from the ceiling, and, on the mantelpiece beside the chiming clock, a Bible and an ABC of trains. There is a noise of trains from outside, and a thin curtain is drawn across the window. The GIRL *enters and looks cautiously round the room. She is perhaps twenty-two, dressed as an office girl with artistic interests.*

The MAN *follows her in and switches on the pale bulb from the door. He is nearly forty, with thinning hair, indecisive good looks, a business suit and a stiff collar. He and the girl are both wearing overcoats. They have no luggage.*

As she looks round the room, the GIRL *begins to laugh gently.*

MAN. Why're you laughing?

GIRL. I don't know.

MAN. You're happy?

GIRL. I laugh when I'm hungry too.

MAN (*disappointed*). If you'd rather eat . . .

GIRL. Not at all. (*She throws her arms round him.*) You look so big in that overcoat . . . like a house.

MAN. I'll take it off.

GIRL. Not yet. What's this place?

MAN. Just a hotel . . . .

GIRL. A hotel?

MAN. By the station. It's convenient. . . .

GIRL. What for?

MAN. The north of England.

GIRL (*dreamily*). You say the most ridiculous things. . . .

They kiss.

And no one knows we're here?

MAN. I'm having a long business lunch with the textile buyers in the Tudor Room . . .

GIRL. And I'm alone with an open continental sandwich in a dark corner of the coffee bar with the rubber plants brushing my cheek and the out-of-work actors staring like hungry jackals at the big Italian waitresses in the small black trousers . . .

MAN. And I'm saying: 'Well, gentlemen, have a large plate of smoked salmon on the Commissioners of Inland Revenue.'

GIRL. But if they looked for us in those places . . .

MAN. They wouldn't find us.

GIRL. No, we're nowhere. . . .

MAN. We're here.

GIRL. We've disappeared . . . We don't exist.

MAN. For an hour . . . or longer!

GIRL. No.

MAN. Business lunches stretch out endlessly.

GIRL. You can't spend much time on an open continental sandwich.

Pause.

MAN. You look so small in that overcoat.

GIRL. What do I look like?

MAN. A child in the park on a snowy morning. A woman who's disguised herself to run away to sea. . . .

GIRL. Go on talking. . .

MAN. The inexperienced wife of an Arctic explorer. . . .

GIRL. Go on!

MAN. I've run out.

GIRL. What of?

MAN. Words.

Pause.

GIRL. As a matter of fact they're quite good, those sandwiches. And they have other things, too, hamburgers, hot franks in soft floury rolls, great rubes of mustard. Such up-to-date and convenient food!

MAN. You'd rather be in the coffee bar?

GIRL. This is much more . . .

MAN. What?

GIRL. Exciting.

MAN. You mean that?

GIRL. Because I love you.

MAN. And me!

GIRL. How long?

MAN. Since the day you walked into my office . . .

GIRL. With the new design for bedspreads.

MAN. Spanish ivy!

GIRL. You remember!

MAN. And said: 'Is this the way to the duplicating department?'

GIRL. And you said, 'No.'

MAN. But I'd show you. . . .

GIRL. And you rose up with the light from the window behind you so you appeared all silver, like a shining statue . . .

MAN. And I took you to Mr Jevons . . .

GIRL. Down the long dark corridors, past the rude and elderly stares of the typing pool . . .

MAN. In the lift.

GIRL. You didn't say a word!

MAN. We certainly established sympathy. . . .

GIRL. You being so quiet in the lift was what I appreciated. Not saying any vulgar remark such as 'Where have you been all my life?' or 'Is there another one at home like you?' Not even looking. . . .

MAN. I was genuinely impressed!

GIRL. Yes.

MAN. And you seemed so lost and uncertain. Like I sometimes feel in that great organization.

GIRL. What words . . . from the head of the textile buying department!

MAN. Only the policy director.

GIRL (*holding on to him*). Oh, love! How it attacks you!

MAN (*thinking of his work*). I'm only the Number Two in that slow-moving department. Blast Harris!

He kisses her almost absent-mindedly, and she breaks away from him.

GIRL. You don't think I'm the sort of girl who comes to a place like this?

MAN (*giving her all his attention again*). No!

GIRL. Then why'm I here?

MAN. My fault.

GIRL (*shakes her head thoughtfully*). That must be the sort of girl I am.

Train noises.

What's that?

MAN. The station.

GIRL. I'm the sort to come here. (*A thought strikes her.*) And what about you? Is this how all your lunch hours are passed, with some girl or other, and you have to creep out of the office at four o'clock every day for an enormous great high tea?

MAN. I've never been here before.

GIRL. Honest?

MAN. Yes.

GIRL. I'm sorry.

MAN. I love you.

GIRL. Say it again. . . .

MAN. I love you.

GIRL. Yes.

MAN. For six months. . . .

GIRL. All through the summer.

MAN. With nowhere to go.

GIRL. In spite of the office and your . . . home life.

MAN. It kept us alive.

GIRL. When we had only a few moments; standing by the tea
trolley in the corridor.

MAN. Holding hands in the lift. . . .

GIRL. You waiting for me in the Embankment Gardens,
always first out of the office, being on the executive planning
side. . . .

MAN. Always the same bench!

GIRL. With the flowers standing straight as soldiers and the
one-stringed fiddle playing in front of the tube and the
tramps asleep under their sheets of newspaper. We had ten
minutes a day, now we've got . . .

The clock chimes a quarter.

MAN. Three-quarters of an hour.

GIRL (*moving away from him, and round the room*). In this
room.

MAN. You don't like it?

GIRL. It's not all that sordid really.

MAN. We could make ourselves more at home . . . take off
our coats.

GIRL. It's cold.

MAN. I'll light the gas. (*Goes to the gas fire.*) It needs a shilling
. . . (*He can't find one.*) Damn!

GIRL. I'll look. (*She burrows in her handbag.*) Only sixpences.
Would it take two sixpences? (*She puts them in the fire . . .
no gas.*)

MAN. Now you've lost your money.

GIRL. It really doesn't matter.

MAN. Let me give it back to you.

GIRL. It couldn't matter less.

MAN. By the end of the week you'll be short of a coffee.

GIRL. No, really.

MAN. Here. (*Counting money to give her.*) Sixpence . . . sevenpence . . . ninepence. . . .

> There is a quick knock at the door and the MANAGERESS enters. Meanwhile the GIRL is almost shouting.

GIRL. I don't want your money!

MANAGERESS. Did you want something? (*The* MANAGERESS *is a large woman, motherly and concerned.*)

MAN. Ah, yes, a shilling for the gas.

MANAGERESS (*to the* GIRL). You're cold. A journey does make you cold. Much snow up there?

GIRL. Up where?

MANAGERESS. The north of England.

MAN (*hastily*). Just a powdering of snow, didn't you say, darling?

GIRL (*bewildered*). I haven't any idea. . . .

MAN. The train was going too fast to take a good look.

MANAGERESS. An express?

MAN. That's it.

MANAGERESS. They *can* be fast. Was it the *Scotsman*?

GIRL. Was what?

MANAGERESS. The *Flying Scotsman*. My little boy collects engine numbers. Many a time he's seen the *Scotsman*, waiting at the end of the platform. Puffing and blowing. Would you like a cup of tea?

MAN. Not at all.

MANAGERESS (*to the* GIRL). Wouldn't you?

GIRL. Well . . .

MANAGERESS. Isn't that husbands for you? Never appreciate the plain and simple fact that what we wives need after a long cold train journey is a home-made cup of tea. Much snow, did you say?

MAN. She had lunch on the train. . . .

MANAGERESS. That doesn't take the place, dear, does it?

GIRL. What of?

MANAGERESS. A cup of tea. (*She is going.*)

GIRL. Just a. . . .

MAN. Very quick cup.

The MANAGERESS *goes.*

GIRL (*lost and puzzled as she turns to him for an explanation*).
   Where've I come from?

MAN. Scarborough.

GIRL. Why?

MAN. I told her that was where you lived.

GIRL. Why should I live in Scarborough?

MAN. Because you're married to me.

GIRL (*accusingly*). Then why don't you live in Scarborough
   too? What's the matter with you? Can't you stand the climate? You delicate or something?

MAN. I've got digs in London.

GIRL. Thank you very much!

MAN (*patiently*). It's the housing shortage. I've simply got to
   be near the office. So you're living with your mother in the
   north!

GIRL. Charming!

MAN. Naturally, it's a long journey and you don't get up to
   London very often . . . .

   Knock.

   Come in.

The MANAGERESS *comes back with a cup of tea.*

MANAGERESS. Drink that down and you'll feel the benefit.
   You must be worn out!

MAN. She's not very tired. . . .

MANAGERESS. But they *are* a strain. On a long journey. . . .

GIRL. What are?

K

MANAGERESS. Running up and down the corridors. Poking their noses into the first class. Playing with the chickens in the guard's van and locking themselves in the toilets.

GIRL. It's like a sort of dream. (*She sits on the bed, lost and confused.*)

MANAGERESS. Never seen London before? This is their first glimpse of the smoke?

GIRL. What's she saying?

MANAGERESS. Their first tube and double-decker? If I know anything, that'll mean the Chamber of Horrors for you this afternoon, unless their Aunty . . .

GIRL. Is she out of her mind?

MANAGERESS. You know what mine does on a long journey?

GIRL. How can I possibly tell?

MAN. Well, I think you've finished your tea.

GIRL. It's hot.

MAN. You won't want it?

GIRL. Might as well. . . .

MANAGERESS. On a long journey mine always takes out his box of crayons, and chalks the marks of an infectious disease on his face before the journey commences. . . .

GIRL (*puzzled*). What for?

MANAGERESS. To ensure privacy in the compartment. . . .

GIRL (*interested*). Does it work?

MANAGERESS. Nine times out of ten. And if not . . .

GIRL. Yes?

MANAGERESS. He can make it pretty sticky for those that do venture in. But why I mentioned that rogues' gallery was this. When his cousins come on a visit from the north, it's always down the stairs at the Tussauds they make their first port of call. . . .

MAN. Ours don't like that sort of thing. Finished your tea, darling?

MANAGERESS. They don't like Tussauds?

MAN. Gentle, nervous children, weak on history . . . You'll

want to wash up the cup? (*He takes the cup from the* GIRL *and gives it to the* MANAGERESS.)

GIRL. Who are we talking about now?

MAN. Our children.

GIRL (*breathless*). How many?

MANAGERESS (*accusingly*). Three.

GIRL. Three?

MANAGERESS. Two boys and then your husband got his girl!

GIRL. Congratulations!

MAN. Time's passing.

MANAGERESS (*leaving with cup and saucer*). I've got things to do. They'll be excited, though, seeing Aunty after all this time . . . . (*She goes.*)

GIRL. Who's Aunty?

She rises accusingly to her feet. The MAN *tries to kiss her, but she turns her face away. She repeats insistently:*

WHO'S AUNTY?

MAN. My married sister. She lives near the Heath.

GIRL. Is that a good thing?

MAN. It's a godsend, as I told the Manageress. She can look after the children. . . .

GIRL. They're with her now. . . .

MAN. She's quite capable . . . a trained nurse, that's what she used to be.

GIRL. Well, I should think they must be totally confused in their small minds.

MAN. Confused?

GIRL. Bewildered.

MAN. But why? . . .

GIRL. For God's sake. What's it all about? Those quiet gentle little children with no sense of history are woken out of their warm beds at what must have been a cruelly early hour in Scarborough, and dragged all the way to London only to be dumped with some ex-matron of an aunt while we scurry off to a small private hotel in King's Cross! And another thing about those children . . . where are they going to spend the night?

MAN (*guiltily*). I thought . . .

GIRL (*challengingly*). Well? (*Pause, then the* GIRL, *incredulous, says.*) You can't mean . . .?

MAN. You'll all want to get back.

GIRL. To SCARBOROUGH?

MAN. Well, it is home. Only temporary, of course.

GIRL (*rushing to the mantelpiece, she seizes the* ABC *and turns up the pages with bitter determination*). Scarborough. Saxmundham. Scalby . . . Scarborough! Pop. forty-three thousand nine hundred and eighty-five. Early closing Wed. London two hundred and three miles! Four hundred and six miles a day you would laughingly see me travel with three young children who can't be all that grown up and responsible, bearing in mind that fact, which you very well know, that I am exactly twenty-three. . . .

MAN (*miserably*). The boys were twins.

GIRL. You know what! I DON'T THINK YOU'RE FIT TO HAVE CHILDREN! I can't think why you went on breeding, for the selfish reason of wanting a girl after the twins, and, when I've given birth to them and all that, you can only think of sending them on pointless and exhausting train journeys practically the whole length of the British Isles. . . .

MAN. Listen!

GIRL. They'll be dropping asleep by the time we get home, and suppose we can't find a taxi . . . .

MAN. Please, let me explain. . . .

GIRL. Four lives you've got in your hands.

MAN. I was desperate!

GIRL. THEN WHY COULDN'T YOU COME UP AT THE WEEK-END?

The clock chimes the half hour.

MAN. There's so little time. . . .

GIRL. Such inconsiderate behaviour!

MAN. Do we have to talk?

GIRL. I certainly think you owe me an explanation.

MAN. I'm in love with you.

GIRL. You have odd ways of showing it. If that's the way you treat all your wives!

MAN. You're not my wife!

GIRL. That's one consolation.

MAN. We love each other!

GIRL. What about it?

MAN. Let's be thankful! Let's celebrate the revolution! The victory against the dull and unaffectionate rulers of our lives! Look at this room! Look what we've achieved!

GIRL. What?

MAN. A beachhead in a dark grey enemy country! A small clearing in the jungle behind our own impermanent and wobbling stockade. A place on our own! Does it matter what I had to say to win it for us?

GIRL. Sometimes it matters.

MAN. What?

GIRL. What you have to say.

MAN. It doesn't matter.

GIRL. Anyway, I'm curious to know.

MAN. What?

GIRL. How you got us here.

MAN. Later on. . . .

GIRL. No, now! I want to know exactly who I am. I puzzle myself at the moment.

MAN. Well, I was walking along the street and I happened to catch sight of this hotel. It seemed small and . . .

GIRL. Unostentatious?

MAN. So I was faced with a problem. How could a man and a . . .

GIRL. Woman?

MAN. Exactly! Without any kind of luggage . . .

GIRL. We've got no luggage!

MAN. Come here for an hour, in the middle of the day . . .

GIRL. Your only time for adventure.

MAN. That was the problem. I solved it!

GIRL. You did?

MAN. After a little thought. I said we wanted somewhere to talk. . . .

GIRL. To what?

MAN. To talk.

GIRL. It's incredible. . . .

MAN. The Manageress understood.

GIRL. She hadn't got to face the endless journey back with three uncontrollable children . . . Anyway, we could have done that in the lounge.

MAN. What?

GIRL. Talked.

MAN. No privacy.

GIRL. Or at your married sister's . . . the one who lives up by the Heath.

MAN (*hesitatingly*). Well, no . . . we went into that. It wasn't at all a practicable idea.

GIRL. Why not?

MAN. Well, there's no point in digging up that old buried hatchet.

GIRL. What?

MAN. You see, you've never got on with my married sister.

GIRL. Never?

MAN. She stayed away from the wedding.

GIRL. Oh did she?

MAN. Since then there's been a bit of an east wind between you.

GIRL. I'm not surprised!

MAN. Just one of those little failures of understanding that happen in all families . . . It wasn't at all your fault. You certainly did your best. I told the manageress that, but, well, there it is.

GIRL. What a lot you told that Manageress!

MAN. To get the room.

GIRL. I suppose so.

MAN. All for that.

GIRL. Yes-s. (*She looks at him, long and searchingly.*)

MAN. Because I honestly loved you. (*He kisses her.*)

GIRL (*absently*). Yes. . . . (*She breaks away from him suddenly.*) What's she got against me, anyway?

MAN. Who?

GIRL. Aunty.

MAN. Nothing.

GIRL. What kept her away from the wedding then?

MAN. Well, you know how people are, old-fashioned ideas.

GIRL. You mean you *told* her?

MAN. What?

GIRL. About this afternoon?

MAN. Where have you got me now? (*He looks at her in confusion.*)

GIRL. Where've you got yourself? Do you ever stop to ask yourself that? I mean, whose side are you on anyway? Hers or mine?

MAN. Yours, of course. . . .

GIRL. Well it doesn't look so very much like it! Keeping up such friendly relations with a woman who wouldn't even condescend to turn up at the reception my father can ill afford, leaving our children to the tender mercy of this starched and creaking old matron with her grey moustache and celluloid cuffs who treats me (*She is crying.*) like a nasty mess in the out-patients! I should have thought you might show a little more honesty and integrity and act more like the bright shining husband in glittering armour that you let me think you were when you tricked me . . .

MAN. I tricked you?

GIRL. You let me believe I was the only thing that mattered in your life.

MAN. You are!

GIRL. Now it seems any old aunt gets more consideration . . .

MAN. IT'S NOT TRUE!

GIRL (*a pause. She is sobbing in his arms*). I'm sorry.

MAN. I'm sorry too.

GIRL. You are?

MAN. I'm sorry we had to have all these . . . complications.

GIRL. I didn't mean you tricked me.

MAN. I know you didn't.

GIRL. I just thought you might write to her, that's all.

MAN. Write?

GIRL. Nothing abusive, of course, nothing to bring us down to her level.

MAN. Whose?

GIRL. Just, 'In view of your attitude, it would no doubt be more convenient if you let at least twenty years elapse before paying your first call,' You never wrote her a line like that?

MAN. Hardly. Because . . .

GIRL. You never came out in the open in support of me?

She moves away from him.

MAN. Because . . .

GIRL. And who is she anyway? (*her anger returns.*) Trained nurse! What's that? Florence Nightingale? Madam Curie? What's her great achievement? Rolling up some royalty in a blanket bath? Being present at the removal of a so-called appendix from a so-called film star in a nameless Nursing Home in Hammersmith? I know those trained nurses! Heartless! Knit and gossip all night and drink cocoa in the face of death! Just let her try and hold down my job which isn't just automatic and calls for some creative imagination! We do two hundred versions of the Spanish Ivy pattern now . . . and not one of them a repeat!

MAN. I know.

GIRL. Well, you should appreciate that.

MAN. Don't worry about her.

GIRL. Why not?

MAN. She's not real. . . .

GIRL. She's real to me! Snobs! That's one thing we don't tolerate in our family, thank God. That's one type of person that just seems to me so low that I couldn't get any lower if I got down on my stomach and wriggled under that door. My father's been an ordinary printer for the best part of thirty years, but there's only one type of person that he wouldn't give house room to in any circumstances, and that's a SNOB. Also, he can't put up with the Welsh. But he's never been the sort to go poking and prying into someone's past history and drawing aside his skirts and refusing to attend the ceremony of marriage and turning young children against their mother when her back is turned.

MAN. Look at me!

GIRL. Yes?

MAN. We're alone.

GIRL. Well?

MAN (*urgently*). Remember. Nothing else exists. Everyone else in the world has faded away. All our friends and families and relations. We're alone here together. Fixed and solitary in this moment of time. No one can come near us.

After a quick knock, the MANAGERESS *enters.*

MANAGERESS. I've found a shilling for you! (*She goes to the gas fire and puts it in.*) Now. Who's got a match?

The MAN *hands her a box in silence. She lights the fire.*

There now! That makes it more cosy and homelike, doesn't it?

Pause.

I always say, after a nice coal fire I like a nice gas fire.

Pause.

Of course, you'll hardly be needing all that shilling's worth, now will you?

Pause.

You'll be Good Samaritans to the next occupants.

Pause.

A nice fire is nice to talk by, and you'll want to go on with your discussion.

MAN. Yes.

MANAGERESS. If you give me that change then.

MAN. We had two sixpences.

GIRL (*after searching in her handbag*). We put them down the slot.

MAN. I've only got ninepence, after the taxi.

MANAGERESS (*stonily*). Well, you asked me to get the shilling. I distinctly heard you.

MAN. Yes, we did.

MANAGERESS. Naturally I assumed you had change to give me for it.

MAN. I've got a pound.

MANAGERESS. That's hardly very convenient. How can I change a pound at short notice?

MAN. I don't know.

MANAGERESS. I had to *send out* for the shilling!

GIRL. We've given you a shilling already.

MANAGERESS. What?

GIRL. My two sixpences, straight down the slot, with no result at all!

MANAGERESS. Really . . .

GIRL. You can't expect to get any more out of me.

MANAGERESS. Me? I'm not making a penny! That goes straight to the North Thames Gas Board.

GIRL. With the price of the room, add on two shillings for gas. . . .

MANAGERESS. I've never had any complaints before.

GIRL. How much was the room?

MAN. Well . . .

GIRL. Tell me, how much?

MAN. Two guineas.

GIRL. For an hour!

MANAGERESS. It's no concern of mine if you have to leave after an hour.

GIRL. Two guineas an hour! Forty-eight guineas a day for a broken-down old bed and peeling wallpaper and a gas fire that's daylight robbery and the use of a chiming clock and the ABC of trains! We're in the wrong business! I knew it didn't pay to be creative. . . .

MANAGERESS. I've had twenty-five years in the King's Cross area as a manageress of this private hotel and I've never heard words like that spoken to me before.

GIRL. Well, it's about time. And what about that little boy of yours?

MANAGERESS. What about him?

GIRL. Playing round the station. Going round all the telephones and pressing the button Bs, I should think most likely.

MANAGERESS. I've a very good mind . . .

GIRL. I'm perfectly sure there's some law . . .

The clock is chiming three quarters of an hour.

MANAGERESS. I put myself out to get you a little warmth . . .

GIRL. Some people work for their living!

MANAGERESS. Because you've had a long day!

MAN (*in despair, forcing the pound note on the* MANAGERESS). Take this! Don't come back with the change. . . .

MANAGERESS (*going*). Peeling wallpaper! I tell you, I've had government officials sleep in this very room. Indian gentlemen. And very nicely spoken. Only I was sorry for the fix you and your husband was in. I agreed to take you for the hour. He wanted to talk to you, you see. On a serious matter! WELL HE MIGHT!

She leaves.

MAN (*pause*). I thought we'd never get rid of her.

GIRL (*pause*). Well, she's gone now.

MAN (*pause*). We've only got fifteen minutes left. . . .

GIRL. Now it's coming.

MAN. Won't you take your coat off?

GIRL. I dread it.

MAN. Why? . . .

GIRL. I'm sorry. I know it's silly and stupid and weak of me, perhaps. But ever since I was a child, quite a young girl, you understand, this has been something I have dreaded and I knew it was coming the moment I stepped into this room. I know that was why you brought me here. But whatever good reason you may very well have had, I don't want it to happen.

MAN. But we discussed . . .

GIRL. It's just a horrible feeling I get in the pit of my stomach, just a sick old feeling of waiting and despair. I've felt it coming on and perhaps that was why I was a bit sharp with that old girl, although heaven knows when you have to count every penny, and sometimes travel on the tube with nothing but a cheerful wink at that thin Tottenham Court Road collector, it makes you sick to see money demanded on that exorbitant scale! However, if anyone says to me, 'Could I have a word with you?' it's always and quite certainly the one word I don't want to hear.

MAN. What do you mean?

GIRL. The head designer may say: 'I'd like a word with you in the office,' or my father says: 'We'd like to talk to you if you can arrange to be home early next Wednesday,' or they say: 'This underground ticket looks a bit exhausted, could we talk to you about it?' and I stand and grin and sweat into the palms of my hands, and whatever it is they have to say I don't want them to say it, so please forgive me if all

I can think of at this moment is I DON'T WANT YOU TO TALK TO ME!

MAN. I'm not going to talk!

GIRL. What do you mean?

MAN. You've got nothing to worry about.

GIRL. Why did she say that, then?

MAN. Say what?

GIRL. That you wanted me . . . for a serious talk?

MAN. Please listen.

GIRL. No!

MAN. We've got so little time, and if this goes wrong . . .

GIRL. What?

MAN. What've we got left?

GIRL. It seems I've always got the children. . . .

MAN. Don't you see, you're the one oasis in the desert of my days and night. The one person that's saved me from suddenly growing old and tired among the bright red hang-it-yourself wallpaper and the Scandinavian lampshades and business lunches. So if we have a few minutes . . . don't waste them.

GIRL. No.

Pause while they come together.

I did love you. When you stood up so silver against the light. . . .

MAN. Please. . . .

They are in each other's arms.

GIRL. And when I got out of the lift and a draught of air from the print room blew up my skirt I saw you turn away your eyes and spare me the look of curiosity . . . and I thought . . . here's someone quite exceptional in this building riddled with intrigue and romance. . . .

MAN (*kissing her*). Oh, God. . . .

Pause.

GIRL. What were you going to say?

MAN. When?

GIRL. I mean, it must have been something of great importance.

MAN. It was nothing.

GIRL. To bring a person all that way on the train to hear it . . .

MAN. Nothing.

She leaves him and stands back from him, looking at him carefully, as if seeing him for the first time.

GIRL. I mean, you're not the sort of man that wants a woman to travel all that way just to discuss the weather, are you? It must have been something serious and terrible you had to disclose.

MAN. I never thought . . .

GIRL. And all through that long journey! What about it? Hour after hour, watching the frozen lines, trying to keep the children quiet. All the time the thought going round in my head . . . he's got something to tell you. What's it going to be? What's so bad it can't be stuck in an envelope or said out over the telephone? Are you the sort of man that would keep a woman in suspense like that?

MAN. Of course not.

GIRL. But it must be days ago you asked me to come up. How do you think I've been feeling since then. DO YOU THINK I'VE HAD MUCH SLEEP? DO YOU CARE?

MAN. Don't you understand?

GIRL. Not yet. You haven't told me yet. Let's face it now. Let's get it out of the way at last!

MAN. There's nothing to say.

GIRL. Or are you the sort of man that would bring his wife all this way to tell her something of great importance which might affect their whole lives, and then shut up as tight as an oyster the moment he was in her presence?

MAN. No!

GIRL. Coming to look at you clearly with the light in front of you, I think that's the sort of man you might be.

MAN. I'm not, Listen!

GIRL. Because it can only be one thing, can't it? For me to have come all this way to hear it, it can only be one logical thing.

MAN (*interested in spite of himself*). What?

GIRL. That we're finished. That it's over. You don't care about us any more. Oh, it was very convenient for you, having me tucked away at the end of a long cold railway line! It gave you plenty of scope to cultivate your friendships in the office. To take girls down in the lift and lure them into strange hotels during the lunch hour. You were able to take full advantage of the two hundred and three miles you so carefully put between us. So now you'll write a letter starting, 'No doubt this will come as a terrible shock to you . . .' which you want me to hand in to give you your so-called freedom. Isn't that what it all comes to, if you had the courage to put it into words?

MAN. I never thought of that!

GIRL. Yes, you did. When you started to talk to the Manageress! When you told her the story. The story had to end, didn't it? Can you think of a different ending?

MAN (*after thinking*). There must be one, somewhere.

The clock begins to chime.

GIRL. Two o'clock. It's over. (*She looks at him with tenderness and pity.*) You should never have explained our presence.

She is going through the door.

MAN. Wait. Wait a minute. I'll tell you why I asked you to come down. I'll tell you what I wanted to say.

But she has gone.

The MAN looks round the empty room. He stoops and turns off the gas fire.

We never took off our overcoats!

Collect Your Hand Baggage

Produced by the London Academy of Music and Dramatic Art in December, 1961.

The play was later produced on Anglia Television on 29 August, 1963, with Kenneth More as CRISPIN. It was directed by William Kotcheff.

Cast

LIZ
OFFICIAL
SWEEPER
CRISPIN
MICHAEL
SUSAN
BILL
JANE
PADDY GARDEN-KEEPER
TOURIST
MR ROBERT WALSH

Scene: The big hall waiting-room at London Airport. Eleven o'clock at night. Apart from a number of real objects the set should be empty. Lit signs hanging bear the initials of various airlines. A sign 'CHANNEL FIVE' over an exit. A long coffee bar with stools and an urn. An open call box. A hanging loudspeaker through which announcements of the departure of aeroplanes are made periodically during the action. A clock.

As the curtain rises an old man, the SWEEPER, *is clearing the mess of papers, cardboard cups, etc., from the floor.* LIZ, *the waitress, is resting beside her coffee urn. An* AIRPORT OFFICIAL *in uniform is checking a handful of lists, and the* LOUDSPEAKER *is blaring.*

LOUDSPEAKER: WE ANNOUNCE THE DEPARTURE OF OUR FLIGHT NUMBER NINE EIGHT SEVEN TO ROME, NAPLES AND MALTA. WILL PASSENGERS PLEASE COLLECT THEIR HAND BAGGAGE AND PROCEED THROUGH CHANNEL ELEVEN FOR PASSPORT FORMALITIES.

CRISPIN *arrives with his friends. His arrival is noisy and somehow grand.* CRISPIN *himself is a middle-aged Bohemian with thin, blowing hair and a big tweed overcoat hanging open like a cloak. His grey flannel trousers have the air of having been slept in, his brown, rubber-soled shoes are cracked, and for long periods of the play a yellowing cigarette hangs from his bottom lip.*

In contrast, his friends are very young, very good-looking and well cared for. Their names are MICHAEL, SUSAN, BILL *and* JANE.

The girls, looking up at CRISPIN *and laughing, are pretty. The boys are small featured, well cared for and inexperienced. Their ages are between seventeen and twenty. There are no jeans or high-necked sweaters among them. The young men wear suits, the girls have bought grand fur collars for their belted mackintoshes.*

CRISPIN (*halting them by the* SWEEPER, *looking round the silent place, and saying, to no one in particular*). Thank you all for a loyal and lovely welcome!

SWEEPER (*resigned*). You lot again? (*Pause.*) Cold night. Very airy.

CRISPIN. We're young. We don't feel it.

SWEEPER. All right for you in that overcoat. (*He feels it.*) Nice bit of Harris that. Heavy.

CRISPIN. I'm not selling it. Not yet.

> *The* SWEEPER *goes off, following his broom.* CRISPIN *and his friends move over to the coffee bar and are arranging themselves on stools when the uniformed* OFFICIAL *comes up to them.*

OFFICIAL. Where are you for, sir?

CRISPIN (*amazed*). You new here?

OFFICIAL. Why?

CRISPIN. Where are we not for! Now where shan't we go to tonight? Paris, Uruguay, the draughty and pock-marked back of the moon?

JANE (*tired*). Let's not go anywhere. Let's just stay here.

CRISPIN. Do we *look* the sort of people who'd entrust themselves to aeroplanes! Can you imagine *me* hurtling through space?

OFFICIAL. Well, sir . . .

CRISPIN (*patiently*). Haven't they told you yet. Well! (*To the girls.*) He's young!

SUSAN. Don't disillusion him. . . .

CRISPIN. I'll let you into a secret . . . You collect all these people's suitcases and they pile into those noisy great machines, and the Captains roar them to the far-off ends of the runways and then . . . they stop. Dead! And the Captain comes over the inter-com (*He imitates the* CAPTAIN'S *voice.*) 'This is your Captain Rogerson speaking. Now none of us really wants to go flying about the sky, do we? I mean, we're not that mad. So what do you say we kip down here for the night and in the morning we'll all send postcards addressed from foreign parts? . . .'

OFFICIAL. What?

CRISPIN. They haven't told you that? (*Comfortingly.*) Perhaps you're just not high enough up in the organization. . . .

OFFICIAL. Have you checked your luggage, sir?

CRISPIN (*embracing both girls*). This . . . is all the luggage I possess. . . .

SUSAN (*wriggling away from him*). Do you mind?

JANE. I'm Bill's luggage. (*She holds* BILL'S *hand.*)

MICHAEL (*sarcastically*). How sweet!

> CRISPIN *looks dashed for a moment, then he claps the* OFFICIAL *on the shoulder and says, reassuringly:*

CRISPIN. Cheer up! Just go on collecting passengers and pretending they're for *some destination!*

> *The* OFFICIAL *shrugs his shoulders and leaves, looking at* CRISPIN *with some pity.*

MICHAEL (*to the* WAITRESS). Evening, Liz, darling.

LIZ. You again. The gilded youth!

BILL. So it is.

LIZ. Beats me why you lot come all this way out to the airport every evening. . . .

MICHAEL. To see you, Liz!

LIZ (*ignoring him*). Coffee?

MICHAEL. Coffee, everyone! Coffee, Crispin?

CRISPIN. What . . . (*He is sitting on a stool, looking suddenly tired.*)

MICHAEL. Crispin!

CRISPIN (*anxiously, to* LIZ). There's a plane for Paris, I suppose, at midnight?

LIZ. The night flight.

CRISPIN. That's what I thought. (*He sounds depressed.*)

SUSAN. Not *going* on it, are you?

CRISPIN. Of course not!

LIZ. Here. Five coffees . . . Sugar's beside you.

JANE. I'll have a doughnut . . . .

SUSAN. You'll get fat!

JANE. I don't care if I get fat. It's not important if I get fat!

SUSAN. Why's it not important? (*To* BILL.) Why does she say it's not important, for heaven's sake?

BILL. Don't ask me. Two doughnuts.

JANE (*smiling gratefully at* BILL). Thanks.

CRISPIN (*looking up at the clock*). Quarter past eleven! They weren't quick enough turning us out of the Black Horse.

MICHAEL. They're getting lazy.

CRISPIN. They should turn us out of there at half past ten so that we can drink in the Running Dog until eleven. They didn't give us any time for the second pub, letting us linger on like that. . . .

SUSAN. Tomorrow we'll have to create an ugly scene. . . .

MICHAEL. Make them *throw* us out.

JANE. I don't see it makes all that difference.

SUSAN. What?

JANE. What pub you're in. . . .

MICHAEL. What's the matter with her this evening?

CRISPIN. She's tired of life!

JANE. Just tired of pubs.

CRISPIN (*to* JANE). I know. You want to settle down with last month's *Woman and Joy* and darn socks with an electric machine and swig great gulps of cocoa with your feet relaxed on an old upturned ironing board . . . You're tired of being young. . . .

All except JANE *laugh.*

JANE. Why not?

CRISPIN. Being young's the last thing you should want to relinquish!

JANE. And I don't see what's so special about having coffee in an airport every night. Why can't we have it in a coffee bar. Like anyone else?

SUSAN (*horrified*). With *rubber* plants?

MICHAEL (*horrified*). And glass cups. . . .

BILL (*horrified*). And those terrible hissing machines. . . .

CRISPIN (*horrified*). And people who just came there to *drink coffee.*

JANE. At least we shouldn't have so far to drive home.

CRISPIN (*turning to* SUSAN). You see . . . in another month she'll take the final examination. She'll be committed to using coffee bars for coffee and airports for trips with the kids to the Costa Brava. . . .

> JANE *eats her doughnut.* BILL *bends down and kisses her ear. They whisper together through the talk of* CRISPIN, MICHAEL *and* SUSAN.

MICHAEL. We shan't *all*!

CRISPIN. All of you!

MICHAEL. You escaped. . . .

CRISPIN. Me?

SUSAN. You did, Crispin. You really did.

CRISPIN (*gloomily*). Thanks.

MICHAEL. Who was that little old man who came over to you in the pub?

SUSAN. He had gold edges to his teeth. I've never seen that before. Like picture frames!

CRISPIN. He wrote great poems when he was at the University.

SUSAN. How do you know?

CRISPIN. I was there with him (*Short, sad pause.*)

> SUSAN *looks at* BILL *and* JANE.

SUSAN. Stop snogging!

> JANE *holds out her hand for inspection.*

JANE. *Look!* What he's given me.

SUSAN. It's a wedding ring!

BILL (*apologetically*) We've used it before. . . .

JANE. But it's a presentation (*Doubtfully, to* BILL.) It *is* a presentation, isn't it?

BILL (*holding her hand*). Yes. (*Then apologetically, to the others.*) She gets these mad ideas. . . .

JANE. It's to announce our engagement.

SUSAN. It's quite moving . . . in an obvious sort of way.

MICHAEL. It's not *serious?*

JANE. Why not?

CRISPIN. Well, you're doing it wrong . . . A wedding ring ought to be fumbled for, in church, from what I remember.

MICHAEL. A sad ceremony?

JANE. Why shouldn't we get married? People do it . . . all over the place.

BILL. I know it *sounds* obvious, but it might turn out rather unusual!

JANE. After the finals, I mean, we must do something . . . We need a home. . . . (*To* MICHAEL.) We can't go on borrowing your room in the afternoons for all eternity. That studio couch. With the springs falling out of it. . . .

BILL. While you and Susan go and sit in the Baker Street Classic. . . .

> *Their words have been rising in speed and excitement, until* CRSIPIN *says suddenly in a gloomy voice :*

CRISPIN. Marriage!

BILL. You're against it?

CRISPIN. It's like a journey, by air! To go to the airport is the best way of spending the evening! But to take off is . . . merely vulgar!

JANE. You never married?

CRISPIN. I won't say never.

JANE. Where is she?

SUSAN. Your dark secret. . . .

MICHAEL. You never told us.

SUSAN. Tell, Crispin . . . tell, tell.

A LOUDSPEAKER: 'WE NOW ANNOUNCE THE DEPARTURE OF OUR FLIGHT NUMBER FIVE O FOUR TO ATHENS AND TEHERAN. . . .'

SUSAN. The East . . . (*She puts a paper table napkin like a yashmak round the bottom of her face, her eyes peering large and Eastern above it.*) You met her in the Cas-Bah!

MICHAEL. On the way home from that drunken orgy with the British Ambassador. . . .

SUSAN. She was being auctioned in aid of the Turkish Red Cross. . . .

MICHAEL. And you put in a small bid.

CRISPIN (*shaking his head*). We met in Eastbourne. Her name was Marigold. . . .

JANE. Eastbourne!

BILL. Honestly, Crispin, more of your past emerges . . .

SUSAN. Whatever were you doing in Eastbourne? Don't tell us.

CRISPIN. Why?

SUSAN. It's bound to be something . . . disgusting!

LOUDSPEAKER: 'PASSENGERS ON FLIGHT FIVE O FOUR WILL PLEASE COLLECT THEIR HAND BAGGAGE AND PASS THROUGH THE CUSTOMS. . . .'

CRISPIN. I'd just come down from the University. My father, the late Admiral, had inconsiderately died at Malta leaving me nothing but his collection of oriental butterflies.

BILL. Parents!

CRISPIN. Faded moth-eaten creatures, stuck through with pins. . . .

> *During the following speech* MICHAEL *and* SUSAN *are not listening but are whispering, their heads together.*

All my friends, even the small dim ones with mackintoshes, seemed to have slipped into employment, jobs were kept

warm for them in various concerns and embassies. But . . .
there was no niche for me! I had to teach English. . . .

MICHAEL. What?

CRISPIN. To French boys in Eastbourne. With long green
plus-fours and cigarettes cupped in the palms of their yellow
little hands.

SUSAN. Who were?

CRISPIN. What I taught. The parents sent them to Eastbourne which they thought was reassuringly like Le Tou-
quet. The boys got up to no good in the public gardens and I
got . . . married.

He looks sadly up at the clock, and says to LIZ:

If anyone was catching the plane to Paris . . . I suppose
they'd be here by now?

LIZ. The bus comes in about five minutes.

CRISPIN. Five minutes. . . .

BILL. Tell us, Crispin, about married life.

CRISPIN. It didn't last. The *plates* finished me.

SUSAN. Plates?

CRISPIN. Side plates. (*He orders more coffee.*) Coffee! Coffee
to celebrate the engagement. Cups of cold coffee . . . with
cigarette ends in the saucers.

BILL. I'm depressed.

JANE. Why?

BILL. Marriage! You see what happens to it.

JANE. What?

BILL. It crashes . . . on the side plates. Ask Crispin!

CRISPIN. Marigold had a little . . . capital, you see. She
came up to London and opened something called the Wee
Gnome Tea Shop. The plates were all so small. Gnome size.
There was no room on them for a substantial meal in the
evenings!

SUSAN. So you left!

MICHAEL (*laughing*). Because of the plates!

SUSAN (*admiring*). No one else would leave for that sort of reason.

MICHAEL. Only Crispin! The free man!

LIZ *hands round coffee.*

CRISPIN. Could I ask you to credit my account?

JANE. I'll pay . . . (*She produces money.*) Only . . . wish me luck.

CRISPIN (*raising his cup of coffee*). Your health!

JANE. You don't mean it. None of you mean it!

CRISPIN. I said it. You can't expect me to mean it as well.

MICHAEL. He can't mean everything he says.

JANE. We're getting married.

BILL. When I've finished my exams.

JANE. You gave me a ring.

BILL. Only don't make such a great thing of it.

JANE. Why not? Why shouldn't we announce it in the papers and start a mortgage and go on a honeymoon to Paris on the night flight like . . .

LOUDSPEAKER: 'WE ANNOUNCE THE DEPARTURE OF FLIGHT NUMBER THREE O SIX TO MANCHESTER. WILL PASSENGERS COLLECT THEIR HAND BAGGAGE.'

CRISPIN. Side plates! Often with scones on them, left over from the afternoons. And the Wee Gnomes themselves, to hold the salt and pepper . . . and the cold polished floors with only a gaily coloured hand-made rug to skid about on. And Marigold with a crumpled handkerchief in the pocket of the peasant smock she wore so that you had no idea of the shape she'd been born with.

SUSAN. Marriage!

CRISPIN. It wasn't for me. Now I'm free. The whole world is – available. I do what I like and feel, oh, as if I still had time to spare before my final exams!

JANE. I wish I did.

CRISPIN. No home. Only a nice independent room in Gloucester Road.

MICHAEL. How's that landlady?

JANE. With the unbelievable name.

CRISPIN. Mrs Garden-Keeper, the sprightly widow of an
Indian Civil Servant? Quite well, and so is her daughter
Paddy. Paddy Garden-Keeper . . . (*He laughs.*) Isn't it a
wonderful name? As a matter of fact she reminds me a
little of the long-lost Mrs Crispin. I get the same feeling
of guilt when she blows her nose. That sad work with the
handkerchief!

They laugh.

Show some respect. For the woman I live with!

SUSAN. Crispin, you don't!

CRISPIN. Only in her dreams.

SUSAN. Poor girl! I bet she dreams continually.

CRISPIN. What else can she do? She spent all her early
emotional years in jodhpurs and now she's deprived of her
horse.

JANE. Why?

CRISPIN. No room in the flat, and the cost of oats has been
out of the question since Daddy died. So she sits at home in
the evenings, her thoughts full of the triumph of forgotten
potato races in long-distant gymkhanas. She closes her eyes
and she's a child again, riding round the ring with a rosette
clutched between the wired teeth. . . .

*He takes a flower from the counter and grips it between his
teeth, making cantering motions on his bar stool.*

JANE. Can't she find anyone . . . to take the place of the
horses?

CRISPIN. There's a boy from the travel agency where she
works, but I don't think he's greatly interested. She's not a
great pleasure to the eye. . . .

SUSAN (*contemptuously*). Then what can she expect?

CRISPIN. Snob!

SUSAN. What do you mean?

CRISPIN. When you have the social security of that marvellous mouth!

SUSAN (*pleased*). You're ridiculous!

CRISPIN. Spare a thought for the under-privileged.

SUSAN. Like Paddy?

CRISPIN. We spend millions on free walking-sticks, wigs for the bald, and the provision of plastic tobacco pouches for vicars unfrocked through no fault of their own, but what party's committed to seeing that there's a level of basic beauty below which no girl need ever fall?

JANE. Probably the Liberals.

SUSAN. My aunt's a Liberal.

JANE. They must be committed to *something*.

SUSAN. It's guilt . . . you must have a great guilt about her.

CRISPIN. Who?

SUSAN. This Miss Garden-Keeper you keep on about so. . . .

CRISPIN. Guilt? (*He looks at the clock.*)

SUSAN. Why does it make you feel *bad* . . . That she's not Miss Stratosphere of nineteen sixty?

CRISPIN. Well, I suppose . . . (*He is a little ashamed.*) Last night words galloped away with me.

JANE. They always do.

MICHAEL. Crispin! What *have* you been saying now?

CRISPIN. I said it more to fill in one of those gaps in the conversation . . .

JANE. Those gaps!

CRISPIN. Those long black pauses which are such a feature of life within the Garden-Keepers in Gloucester Road.

JANE. So you had to rush in? . . .

CRISPIN. Imagine it! A cold wet Thursday night and I was kept from meeting my friends by the embarrassing lack of a bus fare . . . My heart was in my damp suéde shoes that'd gone soggy on the way home. . . .

He comes out of his mood of depression and enters a rising mood of hilarity as he begins to act the scene which occurred the night before. First he arranges JANE *on her stool.*

There was my landlady . . . Mrs Garden-Keeper.

JANE. Me?

CRISPIN. Sitting by the wireless set and wondering if it'd be beneath her station to attack the meter with a knitting needle for the price of a small gin in the warm local. And *there* was I . . .

He arranges himself and looks bored.

Wondering if I could hope for any luck that evening, like a half-crown found dropped in the turn-ups of my trousers . . . And *there* was Paddy. . . .

He arranges SUSAN.

SUSAN. (*surprised*). Me?

CRISPIN. It'll need an act of imagination! Yawning her head off. . . .

SUSAN *yawns.*

Giving us the full benefit of all those carefully straightened teeth. . . . Life, if you call it that, had sunk to a very low ebb. So, just to create a diversion, I crept up to Paddy.

He creeps up to SUSAN.

SUSAN (*imitating* PADDY'S *exaggerated Kensington voice*). Who's creeping up on me?

CRISPIN. And, 'Paddy,' I said . . .

JANE (*in a quavering voice, as mother*). What's that, Paddy dear?

SUSAN (*as* PADDY). Ssh, Mother! Mr Crispin is making a proposition.

JANE (*as mother*). About time!

CRISPIN. 'Let's do something mad, Paddy,' I said. More by way of a joke than anything else. 'Let's get away from all this nothing to do in the evening and suddenly fly . . .'

SUSAN (*as* PADDY). Really, Mr Crispin, the idea! Mummy, Mr Crispin wants me to fly.

JANE (*as mother*). What *does* he think you are?

SUSAN (*as* PADDY). Perhaps he means flee!

CRISPIN. 'No *fly*.' That's what I said. 'Let's go mad,' I said, 'for a change, and go to Paris. When your mother's not looking.'

SUSAN (*as* PADDY). When?

CRISPIN (*not laughing*). *That's just what she said.* And I told her, 'There's an aeroplane, at midnight. I'll meet you at the airport . . .'

JANE (*as herself*). *You needn't have said that. . . .*

CRISPIN (*guiltily*). I can't tell you, those immense stretches of silence. They lead you to say anything!

SUSAN (*as* PADDY). At midnight when?

JANE. Then there's time for an explanation!

CRISPIN. Tomorrow's tonight. I mean I had this bit of conversation yesterday. 'I'll be at the airport,' I said, 'tomorrow night.'

MICHAEL. And what did Miss Garden-Keeper do then?

Pause.

CRISPIN. She looked contented . . .

SUSAN *looks contented.*

And whispered . . .

SUSAN (*as* PADDY, *in a throaty and alluring whisper*). Yes. . . .

CRISPIN. That's almost how she did it. . . .

JANE. And you didn't disillusion her?

CRISPIN. The telephone rang. It was Jackie Henshaw with whom I was once at college. Oh, in the year dot! He had a job in the Home Office and had been searching for me for some time to see if I could lecture on the surrealist movement to the inmates of Wormwood Scrubs . . . I had to rush straight out and find his whisky in his fine Georgian mansion in Belsize Park. It was late after we'd finished talking, and Mrs Henshaw made me uncomfortable on the Chippendale in their draughty great downstairs. In the morning Henshaw gave me a small sum of money, provided I promised not to lecture . . . He said my memories of the Left Bank would lead the prisoners to mutiny. I haven't been back since. No moment to speak to Paddy . . . but as I went out of the door . . .

BILL. What?

CRISPIN. It seemed we had . . . reached an understanding.

Pause. Then he says, reassuring himself:

I'm quite safe. She won't come.

JANE. Why not?

CRISPIN. It'll be a thought, an idea for her to treasure. Like an old pony club rosette. Pressed between the pages of her *Horse and Hound Annual Year Book*. Something for her to take out and sigh over occasionally . . . But (*Again persuading himself.*) she'll never come. . . .

SUSAN. He's right, of course . . . He knows her character.

CRISPIN. If she was the sort of girl to come, would she be the sort of girl to be stuck with Mummy in a small maisonette and nothing but a distant gaze at the young man across the travel folders to brighten up her dark days at the railway bookings counter?

JANE. Well, if I was her . . .

BILL. You're not. Thank God!

JANE. I believe I'd seize the opportunity . . .

CRISPIN. Opportunities are things she's never seized.

MICHAEL. The world's passed her by?

CRISPIN. Ever since she dismounted for the last time. So although she may toy with the idea she'll never act on it.

SUSAN. Rather sad!

CRISPIN. And we'll never refer to it again. She'll sidle past me on the stairs, her eyes turned away, and I'll smile and she'll think I was all ready, tonight, to take her to Paris.

SUSAN. Crispin . . . You're not!

JANE. The deception!

CRISPIN. Not at all. I asked her to come and she didn't. She deceived *me* not turning up like that. After all, it isn't every day I ask a girl to fly to Paris.

JANE. She's let you down?

CRISPIN. We can honestly say so.

   Pause.

It's another of those events that haven't happened, like the flights we go on each evening, to distant parts of the globe.

LOUDSPEAKER: 'WE ANNOUNCE THE DEPARTURE OF FLIGHT FIVE O NINE TO VANCOUVER.'

SUSAN. You sound regretful.

CRISPIN. I'd as soon be flying on that frozen trip to Canada as dashing through the air with Paddy. There's nothing to worry about. *We're grounded!*

JANE. You're safe!

CRISPIN. And the aeroplane, as it always does, can leave without us. . . .

He is about to drink coffee when his eyes become fixed and riveted with horror at something he can see off stage. He slowly puts the coffee cup down. Then he turns towards the bar and buries his face in his hands.

MICHAEL. What is it?

SUSAN. Is he ill?

JANE. The wet . . . shoes.

CRISPIN. It's not the shoes. (*In a terrible whisper.*) It's Miss Garden-Keeper. Equipped with luggage!

PADDY GARDEN-KEEPER, *carrying a suitcase and dressed for travel, enters slowly. She sits at the opposite end of the coffee bar from the group round* CRISPIN *and does not look at him.* LIZ *comes up to her behind the bar, and* PADDY *orders a cup of coffee.*

When it is brought, PADDY *takes out a handkerchief and thoroughly blows her nose. With a look of doom* CRISPIN *leaves his friends and approaches* PADDY. *He sits on a stool beside her. While* CRISPIN *talks to* PADDY *his friends talk, occasionally laughing and whispering together, staring at* CRISPIN *to see how he is getting on from time to time.*

CRISPIN. Hullo.
PADDY (*as if surprised*). Oh. Hullo.

She has a scrubbed appearance and a nervous, Kensington accent. Her clothes are shabby and her shoes need repairing. Her ankles are thick and her nose shines in the hard neon light.

CRISPIN. Surprised to see me?
PADDY. Yes. Rather . . .
CRISPIN. You didn't think I'd be here?
PADDY (*she giggles,* CRISPIN *winces*). Well, not really.

He sits down beside her on a stool.

CRISPIN. You couldn't have thought I'd be so heartless . . . as not to come at all?
PADDY. I know you're not heartless.
CRISPIN. I hope you go on thinking that!
PADDY. Why?
CRISPIN (*taking breath*). Miss Garden-Keeper . . . (*He nerves himself for what he has to say.*) I've got to tell you . . . I know this sounds terrible, but I'm not here for the reason you think. In fact I . . .
LOUDSPEAKER (*booming*): 'WILL MR. EVERARD PLEASE COME

TO THE INQUIRY DESK. MR EVERARD TO THE INQUIRY DESK. MR EVERARD TO THE INQUIRY DESK. PLEASE.'

PADDY (*sneezing*). Sorry. What did you say?

CRISPIN (*deflated*). You've got a cold.

PADDY. Yes.

CRISPIN. You should be in bed. Nursing it, you know. I mean, looking at you I can see quite clearly you're in no condition to travel.

PADDY. I'll be all right!

CRISPIN. Paris is draughty, at this time of year . . . Those wide streets – you can stand by the Louvre and feel the cold wind all the way from the Arc de Triomphe . . .

She opens her case, brings out a guide book and starts searching on a map.

What's that?

PADDY. I'm looking for it. . . .

CRISPIN. What?

PADDY. The Arc de Triomphe.

Miserably he points it out.

CRISPIN. Here. . . .

PADDY. I bought this today.

CRISPIN. I hope it wasn't expensive.

PADDY (*looking at her book*). It must be marvellous . . . the vistas . . .

CRISPIN. Vistas . . . Oh, they're not very much. I mean, personally, give me Hyde Park Corner. . . .

PADDY. You don't mean that. . . .

CRISPIN. I definitely do . . . And in Paris they have this low creeping sort of mist. Very treacherous. With a cold coming on.

PADDY. I've got this muffler.

She pulls a big school muffler across her face.

CRISPIN. I see you have.

PADDY. You see, I'm all equipped. Even down to phrases.

She brings another small book out of her case and reads phrase: 'J'ai une douleur ici dans la poitrine'.

CRISPIN. I don't suppose you'll need that really. . . .

PADDY. I wish I'd learnt more. When I was meant to be at my French Prep I was always volunteering to muck out the stables.

CRISPIN winces.

PADDY. Silly, really. Now I haven't got a pony, but I *am* going to Paris.

CRISPIN. I . . . shouldn't be too sure.

PADDY. What do you mean?

CRISPIN (*desperately*). Weather conditions! On the way out here I thought . . . fog was about to fall.

LOUDSPEAKER: WE NOW ANNOUNCE THE FLIGHT OF OUR NUMBER NINE O NINE TO HAMBURG AND BERLIN. WILL PASSENGERS PLEASE PASS THROUGH THE CUSTOMS AT CHANNEL FOUR.'

PADDY. They *are* flying.

CRISPIN (*looking at her*). And you're excited?

PADDY (*entranced*). I don't feel asleep!

CRISPIN. I see.

LIZ (*coming up the bar*). Coffee, dear?

CRISPIN. Have another coffee?

PADDY. It seems so long waiting.

CRISPIN. You don't know . . . how long it can be. (*He fumbles in his pockets.*) . . . Have you got any change?

PADDY (*looking at him but not in her bag*). No I haven't.

She seems, as she says this, drugged with happiness and remote.

CRISPIN. Excuse me. . . .

He goes back along the bar to the group of his friends. They begin to question him eagerly :

SUSAN. Did you tell her?

MICHAEL. We waited for the tears. . . .

JANE. The screams of rage.

SUSAN. A woman scorned . . . And attacking you with a plastic butter-knife.

CRISPIN. Two bob.

MICHAEL. What?

CRISPIN. Lend it me for the coffee.

SUSAN (*accusingly*). *You haven't told her yet!*

CRISPIN. Well, it's not easy! You can't just blurt out, 'I didn't mean it. Go home to your mother. We're not going anywhere.' You can't just drop a bomb on her like that!

JANE. You're slipping! Where's that ruthless approach?

SUSAN. Of the man who walked out of marriage owing to the shape of the supper plates!

CRISPIN. Good heavens! I'm not getting involved. I'm not *taking* her anywhere . . . It just requires . . . a little *finesse*! That's all it just requires. And two bob!

He takes it quickly from a pile of money BILL *is playing with on the counter, and goes back to* PADDY. *He sits beside her and they drink coffee.*
Pause.

Those are my friends. . . .

PADDY. Oh, yes?

CRISPIN. You may think they look rather young. . . .

PADDY (*looking at them*). The girls seem to be dressed . . . for the Polar Regions.

CRISPIN. Oh, they're not going anywhere.

PADDY (*frowning*). What're they doing here, then?

CRISPIN. Well, they come here every night!

PADDY. What for?

CRISPIN. They don't believe in travel. They just come here for the sake of coming. . . .

PADDY. *I think it's ridiculous.*

CRISPIN. Can't you understand . . . the charm of not travelling. . . .

PADDY. Just . . . sitting here?

CRISPIN. Yes . . . Listening to the announcements, the strange foreign voices.

PADDY. I'd like to hear those foreign voices at closer quarters!

CRISPIN. Look! Go to a bullfight in Seville and shut your eyes and you might just as well not have moved out of . . . Selfridges! Lie on the beach at Capri, and hear the pale typists in their tall flowerpot hats and too many necklaces discuss the weather in Manchester. Mount the Champs Elysées . . .

PADDY (*looking at her guide book*). Where's that?

CRISPIN (*pointing*). There . . . for a jolly good British breakfast and meat-tea snack.

PADDY (*entranced and looking at him*). Can you?

CRISPIN (*thundering on regardless*). But stay here, just here, for a strong feeling of strangeness and the low meaningless murmur of love . . . LOOK!

CRISPIN *nods to where, down the bar,* BILL *and* JANE, *and* MICHAEL *and* SUSAN *are whispering in pairs.*

PADDY. I've never been abroad!

CRISPIN. Preserve your illusions intact!

PADDY. How do you mean?

CRISPIN. Shut your eyes.

She shuts them. CRISPIN *goes on, in a soft voice:*

You're in a gondola, floating through the warm velvet night down the *Canal Grande.* (*He gives it the full Italian pronunciation,* Canal Grand – ay.)

PADDY. Am I?

MISS GARDEN-KEEPER'S *eyes are shut*, LIZ, *passing down the bar with a wet cloth to wipe it, looks at her with surprise.*

CRISPIN. The gondolier gives his little warning cry as you come round the corner of a crumbling palace. 'Owl!' Then he sings. . . .
(*Singing*) 'Santa Lucia . . .
    Santa . . . Lu . . . ci – ah!'
Enjoying the holiday?

PADDY (*thoughtfully*). Mmm, yes. I suppose so.

CRISPIN. But if we were really on that Grand Canal we'd be in a constant state of anxiety about the pound a minute the small craft was liable to be costing. Your dinner would no doubt have been an unappetizing fish sliced into hard rubber teething rings which would be sitting uneasily on your stomach. Mosquitoes would be dive-bombing your unprotected extremities. . . .

PADDY (*opening her eyes*). Oh!

CRISPIN. I should be tipping the boat to feel in my pocket in case the travellers' cheques had been extracted by some pool-eyed child on the Bridge of Sighs, and we should both be longing for the safe, cheap top of a bright red bus.

PADDY. We should?

CRISPIN. That is, if we'd both set out together.

PADDY. But we're not going to Venice. . . .

CRISPIN. Thank God for it!

PADDY. Paris!

CRISPIN. It's the same.

PADDY. I get the feeling that you don't want me to leave the country.

CRISPIN. You see! You hardly know me. . . .

PADDY. I know you quite well.

CRISPIN. You've seen me on your home ground . . . that comfortable little apartment with its fine framed photographs of the various horses in your life!

PADDY. You cheer Mummy up. She's always said so.

CRISPIN. I add colour to your lives?

PADDY. When you wear that big tweed overcoat Mummy says you remind her of – Ronald Coleman.

CRISPIN. Who?

PADDY. Apparently he was a film star. Sort of years ago. I believe she's fallen.

CRISPIN. Who?

PADDY. Mummy.

CRISPIN. Well, at one time your mother must have been quite an attractive woman. . . .

PADDY. In India Daddy had all sorts of trouble with her.

CRISPIN. That's where you were born? . . .

PADDY. I was a child. I remember running away from my nurse and picking up a lot of little bright red seeds. They sent me home when I was twelve, because of the climate bringing me on too suddenly.

CRISPIN. They got you back in time?

PADDY (*laughing*). Don't worry.

CRISPIN. But I'm trying to tell you . . .

PADDY. What?

CRISPIN. Perhaps I amuse you, provide a breath of fresh air. Something different from your life at the pony club. Something that you don't meet among the workers at the travel agency, or your mother doesn't encounter cramming little black cocktail dresses all day on intractable females with the outsize look.

PADDY (*thoughtfully*). No. . . .

CRISPIN (*taking no notice of her*). But get me abroad and how my character might change! Give a man a passport and a limited amount of currency and new sides emerge. He becomes very mean, and continually takes you out for lunch which is no more than a shared portion of *pommes frites*. Or he becomes very truculent and creates embarrassing scenes with taxi drivers which lead to the intervention of the police.

Or a great interest in love revives in him. He drags you to ruinous night clubs where the undressed girls quiver and glow like tall white fish in an aquarium. And in the end he makes contact with a visiting Swede and leaves you with the bill unpaid in a high, unheated bedroom with a poor view of the Gare du Nord.

PADDY. I wouldn't worry you'd turn out like that.

CRISPIN (*disappointed*). You wouldn't?

PADDY. I think you'd stay with anyone. . . .

CRISPIN. Whatever makes you think that?

PADDY. Mummy worries about you, of course.

CRISPIN. She does?

PADDY. She wonders how any man can make do on one pair of shoes.

CRISPIN (*looking at them*). These shoes!

PADDY. But I didn't worry about you until . . .

CRISPIN. Until what?

PADDY. I saw your friends were all young people.

CRISPIN. But I cultivate that fresh, new generation!

PADDY (*looking at the clock*). The time creeps on slowly!

CRISPIN. But it's time for me definitely to tell you . . .

PADDY. Why are all your friends as *young* as that?

CRISPIN. You don't like them?

PADDY. I've never been introduced.

CRISPIN. They're young. They look splendidly well, and I can't tell you the weekly wages their parents pass into their indifferent hands by way of pocket money. They're the sort of circle I've always had, at the University.

PADDY. But you've left the University, years ago.

CRISPIN (*disregarding her*). They hold the moment . . . between growing up and dying, which occupies the rest of our years . . . like a pause. Before they pass their exams and get married and start putting down on a little house.

PADDY. *They* do!

She looks at them. MICHAEL *is now carefully balancing a paper cup on his forehead. The others are watching him without rapture.*

CRISPIN. The only years when we see things clearly. When we have the courage of the anarchy within us.

PADDY. I like men . . . a few years older.

CRISPIN. You're flattering me!

PADDY. I didn't mean that. I meant . . . I like them when they start to plan the mortgage. . . .

CRISPIN. Now that is a stage I have to reach. Thinking of the rent's quite enough. (*Hastily.*) Although, your mother's quite safe.

PADDY. Perhaps you cling too hard to those years, Mr Crispin.

CRISPIN. What?

PADDY. Wouldn't it be more comfortable to mix with friends of your own age?

CRISPIN (*looking at her hard*). That's the way it strikes you?

PADDY. Not that it's my affair.

CRISPIN. You've thought about this.

PADDY. Hardly at all.

CRISPIN. But what you say may show some perception.

PADDY. I just thought I might say it, seeing that you're here.

CRISPIN. Yes. I'm here. I'll tell you this, now we've reached such a high pitch of almost unendurable honesty. I shouldn't be here. I should be at home!

PADDY. Only with older friends, I suggested.

CRISPIN. I should never have said what I've said to you.

PADDY. Oh, don't worry. I expect you have to show off your anarchy or something.

CRISPIN. The things I've said, that'd better be forgotten.

PADDY. And Mummy loves being shocked; that's why she gets those great long books out of the library, about eighteenth-century tarts . . .

CRISPIN. It's time I told you. . . .

PADDY. What?

CRISPIN. That I've deceived you, in a sense.

PADDY. Why?

CRISPIN. For instance, I'm married.

PADDY. Well, so I should have thought!

CRISPIN (*disappointed*). I thought I gave off an air of freedom!

PADDY. You seem too soft-hearted not to have been married at some stage.

CRISPIN. Soft-hearted?

PADDY. I'd say so.

CRISPIN. I tell you. I left my wife quite brutally. Over a matter of side plates!

PADDY. It takes a soft-hearted person to leave anyone in a brutal manner.

CRISPIN. Look . . .

PADDY. Yes?

CRISPIN. Where did you gather up all this curious experience of life?

PADDY. Well, I've met people, since Daddy died of course.

CRISPIN. Then you must realize. I'm not a suitable person for you to get tangled up with!

PADDY. You've been a perfect lodger.

CRISPIN (*furious*). Perfect!

PADDY. And respectable.

CRISPIN (*insulted*). You'll be saying next . . . I'm quiet!

PADDY. Well, much quieter than that bank manager we had before you . . . who gave such noisy parties. Mummy found a girl quite undressed one Sunday afternoon in the kitchen, making toast.

CRISPIN (*appalled*). *A bank manager!*

PADDY. With the North Country Providential.

CRISPIN. Miss Garden-Keeper, don't let's get side-tracked. I'm sorry I'm married.

PADDY. I'm sorry you're sorry.

CRISPIN. For the effect it's had.

PADDY. On me?

CRISPIN. *On your journey.*

PADDY. Well, I can't see why you being married should stop me going to Paris.

CRISPIN. You don't?

PADDY. I'm sorry about it, of course. But you can't expect that sad fact to keep me permanently in England.

CRISPIN. Have you no moral sense?

PADDY. I don't understand.

CRISPIN. Perhaps . . . they didn't get you away from India quickly enough.

PADDY *laughs.*

But it's no good. My being married is a great barrier. I couldn't face your mother . . .

PADDY. Need she know?

CRISPIN. What?

PADDY. About your marriage?

CRISPIN. She's bound to hear . . . in time. I tell you, I only drifted into it through a gap in the conversation.

PADDY. Oh.

CRISPIN. We were standing on the front at Eastbourne. The French boys of whom I had charge were smoking furtive cigarettes and writing up rude words in the shelter. I'd only known Marigold a week. None of my University friends had written that day, and I was feeling lonely. There seemed nothing for us to talk about . . . the silence was oppressive. So I said 'Will you marry me?' For the sake of a remark. Before I knew where I was, she had fallen against me like a felled tree. The French boys were sniggering at us and I was trying to comfort myself by the thought of the small capital I knew she had in the National Savings.

PADDY. You should have been ruthless. . . .

CRISPIN. What?

PADDY. And pretended you'd never spoken.

CRISPIN (*gets up, determined and excited*). You're right! Ruthlessness is the only answer. It's kinder, in the long run.

PADDY. Of course. Cruel to be kind. . . .

CRISPIN. Say what you mean!

PADDY. And don't speak until you mean it!

He takes a deep breath.

CRISPIN. Miss Garden-Keeper . . .

PADDY. Yes.

His mouth moves soundlessly as his words are drowned by an announcement booming from the loud speaker.

LOUDSPEAKER: 'WE ANNOUNCE THE DEPARTURE OF OUR FLIGHT NUMBER NINE O FOUR FOR ROME, NAPLES AND CYPRUS, WILL PASSENGERS FOR ROME, NAPLES AND CYPRUS PLEASE COLLECT THEIR HAND BAGGAGE AND PROCEED TO THE CUSTOMS ON CHANNEL FIVE IMMEDIATELY.'

CRISPIN. Paddy . . .

LOUDSPEAKER: 'AND WILL MR EVERARD PLEASE REPORT TO THE INQUIRY DESK. MR EUSTACE EVERARD TO THE INQUIRY DESK, PLEASE. THANK YOU!'

While this announcement has been going on, CRISPIN has been inaudibly mouthing, and PADDY has opened her case again and taken out a hat, elaborate, veiled and trimmed with artificial roses.

The announcement finishes and CRISPIN is looking at her with unbearable guilt.

PADDY. Were you saying something, Mr Crispin?

CRISPIN. What's that you're putting on?

PADDY (*laughing*). A hat, of course.

CRISPIN (*appalled*). A hat, for Paris!

PADDY. I'm sorry. I wasn't listening. What were you trying to say, Mr Crispin?

He looks at the hat and sinks down on the bar stool defeated.

CRISPIN. Nothing . . . Miss Garden-Keeper. Hardly anything at all.

Looking at her with guilt and misery, CRISPIN *retreats, back to the company of his friends.* PADDY *is left alone, sitting quietly and wearing her hat.*

SUSAN (*as* CRISPIN *approaches*). What *is* it?

CRISPIN. Her hat. She's bought it specially.

JANE. For Paris.

MICHAEL. The Bois de Boulogne.

CRISPIN. I can't look. Those angry roses glare at me accusingly.

JANE. That does make it difficult for you, I do see.

CRISPIN. Impossible!

MICHAEL. Come on, Crispin!

BILL. Be a bit ruthless.

CRISPIN. But I'm not a murderer, am I? Don't credit me with that.

SUSAN. What do you mean?

CRISPIN. I just can't say 'Take that thing off your head and pack it away', when it represents weeks of overtime with the *Railway Guide* and God knows how many nights of dreaming.

Pause.

JANE. There's only one way out!

CRISPIN. What?

JANE. One decent way of keeping the hat on her head and the smile on her face.

CRISPIN. What is it?

JANE. You'll have to take her.

MICHAEL. It's absurd!

BILL. How can he?

SUSAN. He can't go *that* far.

MICHAEL. With *that* girl. Of all the girls in the world.

JANE. Well, why not?

MICHAEL. She simply . . . isn't Crispin's type of female company.

JANE. He's not going to *marry* her. Just fly her across the Channel!

CRISPIN (*thinking of Paris, entranced for a moment*). The Metro smelling like wet tin, the onion soup by the meat market! (*Then he shakes his head.*) It's impossible. (*He looks at the clock.*) There isn't much time, to explain that hat off her head.

JANE. You'll have to go!

CRISPIN (*doubtfully*). And explain afterwards, that I never seriously meant to take her.

JANE. Why explain?

CRISPIN. I'll have to some time. It's absurd! (*He pauses, then says.*) You have to do something ridiculous from time to time.

BILL. He's going!

JANE. He's got to!

CRISPIN. Paris! I'll hardly remember the way to the Café Flore. And when I get there, they'll ask me to pay for the pile of saucers I crept away from in 1939.

BILL. They may have forgotten.

CRISPIN. They've got long memories . . . the French. I can't go. Possibly.

JANE. Why not?

CRISPIN. Be practical . . . I've got . . . (*He feels in his pockets.*) Nothing at all!

JANE. We'll start a collection.

BILL. For Crispin's journey.

SUSAN. We'll float a loan. . . .

MICHAEL. A loan for the love of Allah. . . .

He limps with his cap. CRISPIN *stops him in case* PADDY *should notice: but in fact she is sitting imperturbable in her hat, not regarding them.*

SUSAN (*with pity*). Look at her. Think what you'd be conferring on her!

CRISPIN. A favour? Yes. (*Self-satisfied.*) It'd be a great favour, there's no doubt about that.

SUSAN. I mean . . . it's probably the only time she'll have that sort of adventure. . . .

CRISPIN. Certainly, the only time. What a thing to look back on. A spell with me, across the Channel! What a memory . . . For the long future in Gloucester Road!

BILL. Perhaps she's got some money?

CRISPIN. You mean . . . go Dutch? (*Pause.*) She must expect to pay. Well, we all have to pay for experience!

PADDY *is now reading her ticket, which she has taken out of her bag.* CRISPIN *approaches her, leaving his watching friends.*

You're reading your ticket. . . .
She puts it away, as if caught in some absurdity.
Well, it passes the time. And it's always as well, when you're going anywhere, to make sure you haven't got a ticket for somewhere else entirely.

PADDY. The agency gave it me, at a reduction.

Pause.

CRISPIN. Of course. Just one, they gave you?

PADDY. Yes.

CRISPIN. And you've got the odd scrap of currency, in case your eye lights on something in the Dior *boutique*.

She takes out a ten thousand franc note.

A great table-cloth of money that'd hardly press you a duck
on the Eiffel Tower . . . still, it might last a couple of days,
if you can keep going on omelettes.

PADDY. You want to know a lot about my financial arrange-
ments.

CRISPIN. Only what you've got set aside, in case you're
stranded.

PADDY. Am I?

CRISPIN. What?

PADDY. Going to be stranded?

CRISPIN. I know in the old days it wasn't thought right to ask
a lady what she had in her purse before she went anywhere,
but we live in a Modern Age.

PADDY. Do we?

CRISPIN. The sexes having become equal.

PADDY. Equal?

CRISPIN. You don't feel it?

PADDY. I like a man to offer me everything . . . on a great
impulse.

CRISPIN (*understandingly*). The meal ordered, followed by
a swift dive through the window of the gents when the bill
comes to be presented?

PADDY (*laughs*). I wouldn't like *that*.

CRISPIN. But it's the thought that counts.

PADDY. Backed up by a little financial goodwill.

CRISPIN. Excuse me a moment. . . .

PADDY. You're going away again?

CRISPIN. Only to say goodbye. To my friends.

PADDY. Oh . . . to *them*.

CRISPIN. I'll be back.

Pause.

Don't you trust me, Miss Garden-Keeper?

PADDY. Trust you? I don't know that I've thought about it.

CRISPIN (*looking at her, moved*). Such faith!

He makes off towards his friends. As he rejoins the group he says:

Really, it's moving. . . .

BILL. What is?

CRISPIN. Such faith. In my genuine offer.

JANE. It's only become genuine in the course of the last ten minutes.

CRISPIN. She believes in me intensely. Whatever happens will never spoil the deep reality of this moment.

JANE. Except your slight lack of funds.

CRISPIN. What a worldly little creature you've become, with the approach of matrimony.

SUSAN. All that touching faith won't pay for your week-end.

MICHAEL. Here. Look what we've collected.

He hands CRISPIN *money.*

CRISPIN (*counting*). Three . . . four . . . five . . . five. Six. And such clean English money. How can you have so much?

JANE. We joined together. For the cause.

MICHAEL. The greatest joke in the history of London Airport!

CRISPIN (*putting the money away quickly*). No! Don't mock it, please. Don't do that. There's a faith over there under that nodding vegetation, which mustn't ever be shattered. How much is a ticket?

JANE (*picking up a brochure*). Paris. Nine pounds nineteen. Night flight.

CRISPIN. Another four in ten minutes . . . it should be possible.

JANE. And what are you going to do when you get there? Drive straight to the nearest doss-house?

CRISPIN (*dreaming*). To the Hotel de la Grande Armée. Third on the right off the Boulevard Montparnasse. Full of brass bedsteads and portable radios and the strong, protective smell of soup. Where they keep the bath taps under lock and key and let your room if you're out for five minutes in the afternoon.

BILL. But the money. . . .

CRISPIN. You know what they are at the Hotel de la Grande Armée? Light fingered! Their palms itch. They can extract the electric razor from an American Action Painter before he's got his baggage unzipped. So when we've been there a couple of hours I slap my pocket in horror and discover . . .

SUSAN. What?

CRISPIN. That the honour of France is stained with another great crime against humanity . . . and someone's knocked off my wallet!

JANE. That you didn't have?

CRISPIN. The illusion will be maintained. The great faith'll be unbroken. And from then on we'll go Dutch on Miss Garden-Keeper's ten thousand francs. Well, it's a small price to pay, for a week-end she'll have all her life to remember. And the sky tonight . . . looks like an invitation!

Pause.

MICHAEL. What is it?

CRISPIN. An idea! Just a moment! Thank God I'm still creative!

He leaves them and goes hurriedly off. SUSAN *looks along the bar at* PADDY, *who has ordered another coffee and is working on her French phrases.*

MICHAEL. He's crazy. . . .

SUSAN. He's going to take her! If only she knew . . .

MICHAEL. She'll think he's mad for her.

BILL. It must be wonderful . . . to be his **age.** And still go on doing such crazy things!

JANE (*looking at him sceptically*). Must it?

BILL (*determined*). Well, yes. I hope I never get dull.

JANE. If I didn't think you were going to get dull . . .

BILL. What?

JANE. I'd leave you. Tomorrow!

> CRISPIN *returns with the* SWEEPER *and talks to him confidentially in a corner down stage.*

CRISPIN. I'm offering you a great opportunity. . . .

SWEEPER. What?

CRISPIN (*taking off his overcoat*). This. At a positively knockdown price. A fine great bit of tweed in which I've often slept and made love and . . .

SWEEPER. You want to sell it. (*He feels it.*)

CRISPIN. Was once used to smuggle a small Sinhalese dancer into the University Debating Society disguised as the late Professor Joad on a certain memorable occasion! It's a garment . . . with history!

SWEEPER. Why do you want to flog it?

CRISPIN. I tell you . . . there's a great enterprise afoot!

SWEEPER. A what?

CRISPIN. I'm going abroad. . . .

SWEEPER (*incredulous*). You!

CRISPIN. I'm taking to the air . . . tonight. When you're sweeping up these old coffee cups and *Evening Standards,* I'll be up in the sky above you! Don't you envy me?

SWEEPER. No!

CRISPIN. Not at all? I'm asking five pounds for the coat.

SWEEPER. There's a bit of weight to this coat. Sort of country gentleman style, it could be termed. . . .

CRISPIN. Wear it at point-to-points. Come on. I need the money.

SWEEPER. I'm not a great lover of abroad. . . .

CIRSPIN. Whyever not?

SWEEPER. Four pounds ten. It's the dogs. . . .

CRISPIN. The dogs?

SWEEPER. Say four pounds.

CRISPIN. What worries you about the dogs?

SWEEPER. If you get bitten in any part of the United Kingdom it's a more or less trivial occurrence. But abroad . . .

CRISPIN. Well?

SWEEPER. You've got to drop whatever you may be doing and have an immediate injection! Rabies . . . It's not safe . . . Not to be bitten by them foreign dogs! Make it three pound ten.

CRISPIN. Quick then. I can't haggle with you any more. . . .

He takes money from the SWEEPER and gives him the coat. As he runs off stage he says:

Insular. That's what you are!

As he runs he jumps triumphantly and gives a small dog-like howl. The SWEEPER, holding the coat, looks after him and then goes.

A FEMALE AMERICAN TOURIST enters and looks round behind her, CRISPIN is following her, carrying her luggage.

CRISPIN. And when you get into London, ma'am, *please* don't forget the Soane Museum. The Hogarths have such strength!

TOURIST (*looking in her purse*). Porter, how much is it customary to tip porters here? I'm not used to your currency.

CRISPIN (*as they disappear*). Not more than two pounds. Don't be taken advantage of.

They go.

SUSAN (*looking after them*). What's he up to now?

MICHAEL. *Something.*

SUSAN. You can trust Crispin to do something extraordinary.

BILL. I don't believe he'll manage it, though.

JANE (*looking at PADDY*). She'll be stood up. You ever been stood up, Susan.

SUSAN. No. But I've stood up plenty of people.

JANE. It must be *ghastly.*

MICHAEL. She's probably used to it.

> CRISPIN *enters waving a ticket in one hand, his other raised in a salute of victory. He goes smiling up to* PADDY.

JANE. He's got it!

MICHAEL. You see . . . something extraordinary. . . .

SUSAN. What do we do now?

BILL. We go quietly . . . and leave the rest to history. What a story he'll have to tell . . . in the pub on Monday.

JANE. I hope it's a happy story.

BILL. It'll be hilarious!

JANE (*putting her arm in his*). Come on. We've really got to stop watching them now!

> *The young people,* SUSAN, MICHAEL, BILL *and* JANE, *leave with elaborate stealth.*

CRISPIN. I've managed it!

PADDY. What, Mr Crispin?

CRISPIN. Something you mustn't know about – oh, in the years to come, perhaps. But now, you can still trust me.

PADDY. Robert!

> CRISPIN *turns round. A young man of great responsibility named* MR ROBERT WALSH *has entered and joined them. He is carrying a mackintosh and luggage.*

MR WALSH. I had to explain it all to Frank. And get away from the parents. Did you worry?

PADDY. Terribly. But I had Mr Crispin to keep me entertained. He kept coming backwards and forwards.

CRISPIN. Mr . . .

PADDY. Walsh. He works at our agency. We're . . . friendly.

CRISPIN. I see.

PADDY. And this is Mr Crispin. My mother's P.G.

MR WALSH. Pleased to meet you. (*He nods at* CRISPIN *nervously.*) I'll get some reading matter, darling. For the air.

PADDY. Don't be long! (*As he goes to the bookstall off stage, she looks after him with love.*) It's almost time. . . .

    PADDY *and* CRISPIN *are left together.*

(*anxiously*). Mr Crispin. You won't tell Mummy?
CRISPIN. No. . . .
PADDY. She's the sort that only likes love in library books.
CRISPIN. I won't tell her.
PADDY. And Robert's parents don't really know. He lives near here. In Staines. That's why we came separately. They think he's gone to the pictures.
CRISPIN. Won't they think it's rather . . . a long epic?
PADDY. A friend'll ring them and say he's staying the week-end. His friend, Frank, from the Territorials. He often goes to him, for the week-end.
    Pause.
You don't approve. . . .
CRISPIN. It's the deceit.
PADDY. Well, you can't expect to enjoy yourself. Not if you go round telling the truth to everybody.
CRISPIN. You understand that!
PADDY. We've saved up for this, a long time. Robert's worked.
CRISPIN. I've been working too.
PADDY. No? How marvellous. What at?
CRISPIN. Harder, it seems, than ever in my life before. Miss Garden-Keeper . . .
PADDY. Yes, Mr Crispin.
CRISPIN. I don't suppose you remember. Last night. We were sitting together and the wireless was on. I made a suggestion.
PADDY. I wasn't listening, I'm afraid.
CRISPIN (*incredulously*). You weren't?
PADDY. With this week-end coming, I had so much to think about. I know you were talking, but when you talk . . . You won't think I'm rude?

CRISPIN. No.

PADDY. It's a nice noise most of the time. Like the music you switch on when you peel the potatoes. I mean, you're not really expected to *listen* to it, are you? I mean, half the time, you don't really expect anyone to pay attention.

CRISPIN. Don't I? I don't suppose I do.

LOUDSPEAKER: 'PASSENGERS FOR OUR FLIGHT NUMBER THREE O SIX TO PARIS PLEASE COLLECT THEIR HAND BAGGAGE AND PROCEED DOWN CHANNEL FIVE FOR PASSPORTS AND CUSTOMS. FLIGHT NUMBER THREE O SIX TO PARIS.'

MR WALSH (*approaching them*). Come on, darling, That's us.

PADDY. Goodbye, Mr Crispin. You won't . . . tell anyone, our secret?

CRISPIN. No.

> *They are going, hand in hand, to Channel Five.* CRISPIN *looks towards the empty bar stools and sees that his friends, also, have gone.*

Not even . . . you.

> *The bar is suddenly a big space, almost empty.* CRISPIN *walks across the big floor. Then he puts his hands in his pocket and jingles money. On an impulse he goes to a call box and dials a number.*
> CRISPIN *telephones.*

Hallo. Is that you? I woke you up? I'm sorry . . . I'm sorry to hear that, Marigold. No, I'm not . . . Really, not at all. Nothing's passed my lips the whole evening . . . except coffee. Purely coffee. Well, when I saw you I said I'd be in touch. I know it was some time last year. But here I am, Marigold. Ringing you again. You see. I keep my promises. I've got a ticket here . . . An air ticket. No . . . perfectly sober, but I wondered if you might care for a holiday. We could sort of . . . share expenses. Paris. It's in France, Marigold . . . from what I can remember . . . a place of great gaiety! Yes . . . Yes . . . I know you're busy. Well, I'm sorry about that time. I didn't know you were serving teas at that hour. I thought they were your friends who might appreciate a drop of something stronger in their cups on that cold day. I was trying to be friendly and hospitable. To join in, Marigold. That's all I was doing. Joining in. Look. Don't hang up. Why don't I come round? For a talk perhaps? There seems to be – no one to talk to. I needn't even stay long. Just – talk a little. Of . . . course. I see. You're tired. Worn out? And a cold coming? All right. All right, Marigold. I'll leave you alone. Entirely alone. I understand. Good night, Marigold.

He puts the telephone back gently, as if not to wake her. He steps out of the call box into the empty bar. He looks for a cigarette in an empty packet and then up to the loudspeaker as it says:

LOUDSPEAKER: THIS IS OUR LAST ANNOUNCEMENT FOR THE MIDNIGHT FLIGHT TO PARIS. WILL PASSENGERS TO PARIS PLEASE PASS THROUGH CHANNEL FIVE. COLLECT YOUR HAND BAGGAGE AND PASS THROUGH CHANNEL FIVE NOW, PLEASE.

Curtain

Methuen's Modern Plays

EDITED BY JOHN CULLEN

David Mercer	*On the Eve of Publication and other plays*
	After Haggerty
	Flint
John Mortimer	*The Judge*
Joe Orton	*Crimes of Passion*
	Loot
	What the Butler Saw
Harold Pinter	*The Birthday Party*
	The Room and The Dumb Waiter
	The Caretaker
	A Slight Ache and other plays
	The Collection and The Lover
	The Homecoming
	Tea Party and other plays
	Landscape and Silence
Jean-Paul Sartre	*Crime Passionnel*
Theatre Workshop and Charles Chilton	*Oh What a Lovely War*

*   *   *

Methuen Playscripts

Paul Ableman	*Tests*
	Blue Comedy
Barry Bermange	*Nathan and Tabileth and Oldenberg*
David Campton	*Little Brother : Little Sister and Out of the Flying Pan*
Henry Chapman	*You Won't Always be on Top*
David Cregan	*Three Men for Colverton*
	Transcending and The Dancers
	The Houses by the Green
Rosalyn Drexler	*The Investigation and Hot Buttered Roll*
Harrison, Melfi, Howard	*New Short Plays*
Duffy, Harrison, Owens	*New Short Plays : 2*
Henry Livings	*Good Grief!*
	The Little Mrs Foster Show
	Honour and Offer
John McGrath	*Events While Guarding the Bofors Gun*
David Mercer	*The Governor's Lady*
Georges Michel	*The Sunday Walk*
Rodney Milgate	*A Refined Look at Existence*
Guillaume Oyono-Mbia	*Three Suitors : One Husband and Until Further Notice*
Alan Plater	*Close the Coalhouse Door*

David Selbourne   *The Play of William Cooper and
                    Edmund Dew-Nevett
                    The Two-Backed Beast*
Johnny Speight   *If There Weren't Any Blacks You'd
                    Have to Invent Them*
Martin Sperr   *Tales from Landshut*
Boris Vian   *The Knacker's ABC*
Lanford Wilson   *Home Free! and The Madness of Lady
                    Bright*

                    *   *   *

Methuen's Theatre Classics

THE TROJAN WOMEN   Euripides
                      *an English version by Neil
                      Curry*
THE REDEMPTION   *adapted by Gordon Honey-
                      combe from five cycles of
                      Mystery Plays*
THE MISANTHROPE   Molière
                      translated by Richard Wilbur
LADY PRECIOUS STREAM *adapted by S. I. Hsuing from a
                      sequence of traditional Chinese
                      plays*
IRONHAND   Goethe
                      adapted by John Arden
DANTON'S DEATH   Buechner
                      *an English version by James
                      Maxwell*
THE GOVERNMENT   Gogol
INSPECTOR   *an English version by Edward
                      O. Marsh and Jeremy Brooks*
BRAND   Ibsen
THE WILD DUCK   *translated by Michael Meyer*
HEDDA GABLER
THE MASTER BUILDER
MISS JULIE   Strindberg
                      translated by Michael Meyer
LADY WINDERMERE'S FAN Wilde
THE IMPORTANCE OF BEING
EARNEST
THE UBU PLAYS   Jarry
                      *translated by Cyril Connolly
                      and Simon Watson Taylor*
THE PLAYBOY OF THE   Synge
WESTERN WORLD